LIVE THE PROMISE
"Take the Oath"

About the Author:

Bodie McCoy was born in 1949 in San Diego, CA. In 1977, he and his wife Barbara met and were later married on the carousel on the Santa Monica Pier. They have eight children, 14 grandchildren and one on the way and two great-grandchildren. They now live in the beautiful western North Carolina mountains enjoying their growing family and continuing to share their work.

Since 1982, Bodie and Barbara have been sharing their unique approach to the Lord's Prayer bringing renewed faith, hope and healing tears to thousands.

Within these pages Bode offers us heart-felt stories, clear insights and simple exercises to help us experience this magical prayer in new, deeper and more personal ways.

Live the Promise
"Take the Oath"

Our Father
Who art in Heaven.
Hallowed be Thy Name.
Thy Kingdom come, Thy
Will be done on Earth as it is in
Heaven. Give us this day our dai-
ly bread and Forgive us our tres-
passes, as we forgive those who
trespass against us. Lead us
not into temptation, but
deliver us from evil.
Amen

A true story of discovering the
Interconnectedness of religions
Within the secret teachings of
The prayer Jesus taught:
The Lord's Prayer

"Live
the
Promise"

By

Bodie McCoy

Cover Design by Bodie McCoy
Cover Photoshop by Marci Raneri
Cover Background scanned by Jeff Grandy

Published by New Genesis Publishing
171 Utah Mtn. Rd
Waynesville, NC 28785

Live the Promise "Take the Oath" by Bodie McCoy

ISBN: 978-0-9797493-0-8

DEDICATION

I dedicate this book to my teachers Richard, Doris and JR.
To my wife, partner and best friend Barbara
And to our eight amazing children,
Tammy, Asa, Tiffany, Ampara,
Jessica, Gabrielle, Shawn
and Azza.
With   all
my   heart,
you are my
inspiration and I
Thank you, thank you, thank you!

SPECIAL THANKS TO
Atona, Christina and Oshala,
for their honest opinions and support.
To our editor Sarah and the contributions of
Walt Disney, J. M. Barrie & the free spirit of Peter Pan.
Thank you one and all!

TABLE OF CONTENTS

8

FORWARD

By Barbara McCoy

As Bodie's wife of 30 years I have lived much of what he shares in this book. As children Bodie and I both passionately believed that there was something special, even magical, about the Lord's Prayer. We both believed that, if you said it right, miracles would happen. We discovered our shared childhood experience of the Lord's Prayer one night in 1982 because of a personal crisis. That was the beginning of the magic that Bodie shares in these pages.

What we have discovered since that night twenty-five years ago is that the Lord's Prayer is far more complex than most of us know. It is the best known, most-often recited of all Christian prayers, and is the only prayer Jesus ever taught. Moreover, the way Jesus affirms our true nature in this prayer activates the subtle, hidden potential of all God's children.

Bodie shows you how this prayer bridges the world's religions. You will see how the seven original expressions of Yoga, as well as the most elemental forms of sacred geometry, are masterfully woven into this amazing prayer. The best part for me, though, is seeing this prayer as a sequence of eight "Heart Dances." When you begin to experience these inner dances for yourself, you will feel your energy centers opening and activating. These Heart Dances will elevate your awareness to help you see yourself as you truly are.

No matter who you are or what your current situation is, this book will help you to realize the promise of the Lord's Prayer. It is the promise of heaven on earth:

Thy kingdom come Thy will be done, as it is in heaven so also in earth. Naturally, as Bodie's wife, I am prejudiced. But consider this: I've chosen to support this quest for twenty-five years when most others have considered it frivolous. Especially, as all the while, Bodie and I have been raising our eight beautiful children.

Following our hearts does take faith and saying the Lord's Prayer daily helps me to find the faith I need to release and heal my past. By doing this, I can come forth to meet each day as God's child. My prayer is that our stories about the power and magic of following our hearts will show how the Lord's Prayer can help you to accept the strength and wisdom of the child of God residing within you. With all my heart, I believe Christ's promise of heaven on earth is now unfolding, one person and one heaven at a time.

INTRODUCTION

"The Promise"

My wife, Barbara, and I have eight children, and people have often asked us why we chose to have such a large family. That question always perplexed me. I never asked it of myself, and my answer comes from such a deep place, that it is hard to put into words. We are not Catholics or Mormons, though we have often thought how nice it would be to have a large and supportive extended family like that. It's not because we feel it is the right or moral choice, either. The issue is not a "right to life," nor out of any sense of obligation to our children. Barbara and I genuinely like being parents.

Before we were married, Barbara told me that she wanted to have a big family, and possibly even adopt someday. I'd never really thought about it. I never imagined what having children would be like before they were a part of my life. I loved Barbara so much, that I would have agreed to nearly anything that was important to her; but I didn't do it for her, either.

As I consider my own personal reason for having so many children, I am drawn back to each of their births. All our children were born at home. My hands were the first to touch them, my eyes were the first to look into their eyes, and this experience is the closest thing I know of that answers that question. When the long wait of labor, Barbara's pain, and my concerns for her well-being and that of our newest child were past, there was always a magical moment as I first looked into their eyes. It was like falling in love for the first time, but more.

I feel so blessed to have shared those first sacred moments with each of them, and now I realize what that magic was. It was promise. Their fresh new little hearts and minds were wide open. Their beliefs and personalities hadn't yet taken form. The loving spirit within them was free to be fully present, and that freedom liberated me to simply be present with them. I believe the promise in them touched and awakened the promise in me. With each of their births I felt renewed, and this is also what I feel when I pray.

You probably already know the prayer Jesus taught, The Lord's Prayer, but did you know it contains an ancient mystical formula for awakening the promise of the eternal magical child within each of us? In 1982, a series of challenging events helped Barbara and me to remember the promise that this prayer aroused in both of us when we were children. But it has taken us nearly twenty-five years to realize this promise as adults.

Jesus expressed it in many ways: "Ask and you shall receive," "Seek first the kingdom of God and all these things shall be added unto you," and "Ye are gods." The meaning of the word prayer is "to ask," but Jesus prefaces his prayer by telling us that Our Father already knows what we need. So, what are we to pray or ask for? In this book I will share the story of how we discovered that the purpose of a prayer is not to ask for anything, but to enter an ultimate childlike state of asking. Mother Teresa described it like this: "Prayer enlarges the heart until it is capable of containing God's gift of Himself."

As we pray this way, we come face to face with the promise of the ultimate gift of God Himself, and it is something like the experience of looking into the eyes of a newborn child. In the presence of such promise our hearts and minds open, our conflicts cease, our illusions dissolve, and the truth of unity is exquisitely apparent. The experience of being fully present has been described in every spiritual tradition with names such as Nirvana, Bliss, Enlightenment, Clarity, and The Rapture of The Holy Spirit. Whatever tradition or name you choose, we all begin our journey to the ultimate human experience by humbly asking in a prayer.

Apparently, the allure of bliss, however, has not been enough to inspire most of us to really ask our most heartfelt questions. The monumental problems that we face today didn't begin with us, but how we deal with them will determine what the future will be, or whether there even will be one. If you are not yet aware of humanity's dire situation, then your own personal barriers are set too high to see over.

These problems began with the illusions and barriers that make us seem separate from one another. Believing, feeling, and acting separately not only causes the suffering that plagues us, they also prevent us from doing anything about them. Fortunately, Jesus gave us some amazing tools with which to change the disposition of our hearts. He warned of this day. It was the first thing he taught. He said to repent, which means "to change"; and now, 2,000 years later, the message is the same. Jesus also expressed the solution to all our problems in just two words, Our Father, and the words that follow those clearly describe how we may realize the promise those two words imply. That promise is what this book is about. My prayer is that we may begin to live as one family so that all children will have the exquisite pleasure of looking into the eyes of their children and grandchildren.

PREFACE

Chances are, you are familiar with the Lord's Prayer. If so, then the prayer you say may be different from the one I will be sharing with you here. That's not because I have translated it differently; it is because Jesus taught the Lord's Prayer twice in the Bible. First, the more popular version is in Matthew 6:9-13. Then, in Luke 11:2-4, a shorter version of the prayer is expressed. The fact that these two are nearly identical, and were taught two years apart, tells us that Jesus was not just offering an example of how to pray, but that he was teaching a specific prayer. As this is the only prayer Jesus taught, we must assume that it is very important.

Most experts agree that the second version of the prayer is the most original or authentic of the two; and this is the version we use, but not for that reason. We use it because of the geometric perfection so beautifully embedded in it. This version of the prayer has seven segments or thoughts, and each perfectly aligns with one of the seven chakras, or energy centers, in our bodies. The agreements between these seven sections of the Lord's Prayer, the seven chakras, and the seven original branches of Yoga beautifully reveal how the pure intent of Jesus' prayer is to awaken us to our true divinity.

If you are familiar with the seven chakras or the seven original branches of Yoga, again you may find some differences between what you have learned and what I will share with you here. There are several schools of thought regarding these, and I do not claim to be an expert on any of them. My interest in these chakras and the original branches of Yoga is in how they illuminate the seven levels of the Lord's Prayer. I have therefore chosen to use the interpretations that do this best.

People often ask if I am aware of the Aramaic translations of the Lord's Prayer, and I am; but what I offer you here has not come from these translations. According to Wikipedia, the online encyclopedia, translation is "the interpretation of the meaning of a text in one language (the 'source text'), and the production, in another language, of an equivalent text (the 'source text' or 'translation') that communicates the same message. Translation must take into account a number of constraints, including context, the rules of grammar of the two languages, their writing conventions, and their idioms." Translators are linguistic scholars. I, on the other hand, am not even sure what an idiom is. As you will see, what I have translated are not the words of this prayer, but the interrelationships between its seven parts, the seven chakras, the seven original branches of Yoga, and the sacred geometry that the prayer contains. I find that, all together, these define and illuminate our divine human gift more eloquently than any other sacred scripture. We are creators, and the Lord's Prayer simply guides us to use this most wondrous gift to the greatest possible advantage of us all.

I do love hearing the Lord's Prayer in the Aramaic language. I don't understand the words, but still they ring so true, like a beautiful song. This song supports my own vision of the Lord's Prayer as a sacred inner dance. I see it uniting the opposites within us. As its first two words, Our Father, imply, the prayer is dedicated to unity. Here is its promise: Let your eye (consciousness) be single, and your whole body shall be filled with light. As the prayer's words are understood by our thinking minds, its rhythmic movements and sacred embedded designs are felt within our hearts. Jesus' prayer literally unites the two opposing hemispheres of the brain into a single eye, or consciousness. Thus, the Lord's Prayer illuminates the spiritual truth of unity within the physical illusion of separation perceived by our senses. God and man, East and West, male and female are the integral parts of the sacred whole and united within us as we pray. This is what I believe Jesus intended, and I have written this book to share this magical way of experiencing the Lord's Prayer.

Part I
The Inner Child

PETER PAN

    I believe, as many people do, that our adult choices are often inspired by events from our childhood. This is certainly true of my relationship with the Lord's Prayer. I believe Jesus created His prayer to heal the wounds of misunderstandings, which the child within us forms, absorbs, and carries forth into our adult lives. My life experiences and my knowledge of this prayer have convinced me that the cooperation of our inner child is vital to our spiritual fulfillment and happiness.

On my fourth birthday, my Gramma took me to see the Disney movie, "Peter Pan," at the old 20th Century Fox Theater in downtown San Diego. I can still feel my heart pounding and my spirits soaring as Peter invited the audience to take his oath. As we all swore together, children, parents, and grandparents chanted in unison; "I will never grow up, I will never grow up, I will never grow up." The intoxicating promise of eternal youth inspires passion, even in a four-year-old.

Later in that same movie a bomb, sent from Captain Hook, mortally wounded Tinker Bell. We watched helplessly as her beautiful light faded. Peter turned to us desperately. "Clap your hands if you believe in fairies." We all did, but Tinker Bell's light continued to fade. Then Peter pleaded, "If you will believe in fairies with all your heart, Tinker Bell will live!" Again, we clapped. This time we gave more, and Tinker Bell's light began brightening. Joyful sounds, sighs of relief, and again an empowering sense of promise filled that great room.

Those were the most magical, liberating, and empowering moments of my young life. The movie touched many young lives that year. Its heartfelt rituals may have even accelerated the course of our human destiny. If that sounds far-fetched, consider how the same children who took Peter's oath in 1953 instigated a global renaissance in the 60's. We embraced peace and love, and many of us refused to go to war. We found our own "pixie dust," sat together in tribal circles, and passed the peace pipe. Eventually, some of us embraced the religions of the Far East. We chose to believe in the innocence of our hearts and to have faith that we could make a difference. As Jimi Hendrix said, *"When the power of love overcomes the love of power, the world will know peace."*

If you still have doubts, ask yourself why Disney, Inc. removed the most magical parts of that classic movie. That's right; Peter's oath to "never grow up" and the healing of Tinker Bell by clapping our hands have been edited out of the movie. Why? I don't know, but our children and grandchildren have been deprived of these wonderfully empowering experiences. Yet, they still benefit. I believe Peter's magic has inspired many to see beyond the dogma of churches to the magical presence of the Christ within, which is the promise of the Lord's Prayer.

A HIDDEN TREASURE

When I was seven years old and preparing for my First Holy Communion, I heard Sister Perpetua, my catechism teacher, describing the Lord's Prayer. She called it a "sacred oath between me and God." I clearly heard her promise, "If you will put your whole heart into this sacred oath, you will know God personally and your life will be magical." Sister Perpetua later denied saying this; nonetheless, it inspired me to embrace His prayer much as I had embraced Peter's oath three years earlier. For a few glorious weeks, I believed that, if I said the Lord's Prayer with all my heart, then my mundane life would become magical. Today, more than ever, I believe this promise is true.

When the sister taught us the Lord's Prayer, I did not remember my oath to Peter Pan. Now, however, I believe that the associations of time, space, form, and event between Jesus' prayer and Peter's oath, heaven and Never Land, and Captain Hook and the Devil made a connection deep within my subconscious mind. To a child, Peter and Jesus have a lot in common. Having met Peter first, how could Jesus, God's Son, be any less real or magical?

When I was seven, praying with all my heart meant being fully present and deeply feeling every word, but my young mind wandered easily. The promise of knowing God personally and having a magical life stimulated my imagination, which made it even harder to concentrate. My thoughts jumped quickly from the prayer to what its magical results would be, but its promise inspired me, and I persevered. The more I imagined, the more determined I became; until one evening, as I was trying so hard to feel every word, my mother walked into my room. She looked surprised and asked, "What are you doing?" I think she was curious about how they got me to sit still like that for so long; but when I told her about the magical promise of the Lord's Prayer, she looked confused.

HERESY

The next day, after speaking with Sister Perpetua, Mom was even more concerned. But later, when the pastor of our church called, she broke down and cried. Monsignor Ott told my mom that what I was saying was heresy. He said that my soul was in great jeopardy, and that her son should get professional help as soon as possible. I learned of this in bed that night, when the sound of my parents' fighting interrupted my prayers. My Catholic mom and agnostic father were arguing at the top of their voices over whether I would receive this help. Dad said, "No," and Mom pleaded with him. Then I heard Dad shout, "I agreed to let you raise our children as Catholics, but I'm not going to let that church tell me what is best for my children." Mom sobbed and sobbed, and I felt guilty.

The next day, and from then on, my mom looked at me differently. Afterwards, I felt less at home, and a barrier steadily grew between us. I assumed it was my fault, but I was just seven and had no one else to talk to. I wasn't having much luck with my prayers, anyway, and I finally decided that the problem must be with God. Believing in Him was making me feel bad; and if He couldn't keep His promise, what good was He, anyway?

Between the ages of seven and twenty-one, I was a poor student, an avid surfer, a hippie, an enthusiastic drug user, a smuggler, and an agnostic. I embraced my father's ambivalence towards God: "Maybe He exists, maybe not; but since He's never answered me, what's the difference?" The mantra "God is dead" seemed to work for me throughout the 60's, until one evening in Hawaii. While mixing business (smuggling) with pleasure (surfing and getting high), in the twinkling of an eye I was changed.

LSD & MACROBIOTICS

When I arrived in Hawaii, after making a nice profit on eight kilos of Mexican marijuana, I treated myself and bought 100 tabs of good blue LSD. I'd been taking those blue tabs almost every day for about a month, when I was inspired to do more. I decided to take the rest; about twenty tabs, all at one time. Imagine a jet plane snagging you as it flies by at supersonic speed. Imagine fighting to stay calm as you realize that what you've just done is going to change you and your life forever, and most likely not for the better. Your fight or flight instincts kick in as the world dissolves. Now you're completely focused on the beast within, which all this acid has unleashed.

When the struggle was over and my illusions had been devoured, I was alone in a pitch-black void. Based on my many previous experiences with LSD, I knew I would never visit my previous life again. I was calm. The beast had won, but now I had to make a choice. I'd seen what happened when people under similar conditions had reached out for help. The good intentions of these inexperienced saviors inevitably led to some kind of hell and asking for help really wasn't my thing. The thought of being institutionalized and treated as if I were mentally ill was much more terrifying than the trip itself. Finally, seeing no other option, I did something truly desperate: I prayed, "God, if you exist, I need you now." Instantly, a loving, warm, and comforting sensation filled my heart with joy and my mind with peace. I never doubted God's existence or His unconditional love for me again.

In three months, I went back to California. The year that followed was long, blissful, and very painful, as I quickly alienated my friends, family, and partners in crime. They worked, went to school, jail, or surfed, fell in love, partied, and got rich and stoned. In the meantime, I read about the Yogis of the Far East, meditated, and fasted, until I nearly died of starvation. Everyone assumed I was strung out on smack, and they all tried to help. Finally, weak as a kitten, weighing just 94 lbs., I fled after my father warned me of my mother's plan to have me committed.

I bought a one-way bus ticket from San Diego to Hollywood where I'd heard there was a macrobiotic study house. Macrobiotics, meaning "large or long life," is a philosophy of living in balance with the opposing and attracting natural forces of yin and yang. Kushi House was a beautiful but old and rundown Hollywood mansion, with a huge formal dining room. Nightly macrobiotic feasts were served to the occupants and their visitors. Afterwards, classes and discussion groups on macrobiotic cooking, Eastern philosophy, Zen, Shiatsu massage, acupuncture, etc. were held in the grand old library and living room. With my past behind me, it was a perfect place to begin my new life.

I arrived at Kushi House with no job and very little money. I was too weak and spaced out to work any kind of normal job; but Caroline, the housemother, took pity on me. For just $50 a month and a little sweeping up, I got two meals a day and an old mattress in the basement to sleep on. I had to share my bed with Cleo, the cat, but I didn't mind; she kept the rats at bay. I remember waking up one morning with Cleo on my chest, with a rat still struggling between her claws. As I write of this, it sounds miserable, but I was so very glad to be there.

Everything that I did after Hawaii was in some way motivated by my burning desire to experience God again, as I had that night after my desperate prayer. First, I tried to emulate the vegetarian Yogis of the Far East. The more advanced Yogis could live entirely on the vital life forces called "Prana." I believe Jesus spoke of this when he said, "*Man shall not live by bread alone, but by every word that proceedeth out of the mouth of God* (Matthew 4: 4)."

I failed to become a Yogi, but at the Kushi House I slowly regained my health. For a whole year, however, I was 70 lbs. lighter than my normal weight of 180 lbs. I didn't return to my normal weight until one day when I suddenly started binging on sweets. I felt so guilty, that I tried to purge afterwards, but I couldn't stop. I gained over 100 lbs. that next year. Almost starving myself to death took a lot of willpower, but there's a big difference between a strong will and a rigid, unbending one. A strong will is developed through our devotion to something that we believe is good, and such strength may be transferred as our beliefs evolve. A firm will seems to be strong, but it comes from our resistance to something we believe is bad; it is brittle and therefore easily shattered.

DORIS

At that point of my life, my will was so rigid and brittle, that one cookie was able to shatter it. It was a very big cookie with lots of chocolate chips; and after eating it, all I could think about was ice cream, cookies, candy, and more ice cream. Even during my heaviest drug use, I was never so obsessed, and outgrowing my new clothes practically before they needed washing was both frightening and humiliating. For the first time in my life, I felt suicidal, and that's when I took notice of some of the people that I knew who were looking healthy and happier. I asked one of these people, Jennifer, what was going on? She said they were all involved in a new kind of therapy, and that the new therapist, Doris, was an amazing woman. Jennifer suggested that I could meet Doris at a party that weekend, and I eagerly accepted her offer.

I first saw Doris sitting across the center patio of an Old Spanish-style mansion. She was in her late fifties and had short, salt-and-pepper hair, a strong, courageous presence, and an aura of hard-earned wisdom. I soon discovered that Doris, like me, also had voracious appetites. She quickly helped me to see mine not as my weakness nor my enemy, but as passion wanting for a healthier and more productive means of expression.

After our first meeting, I embraced Doris' unique brand of Reichian Breath Therapy. Her work was a combination of deep, slow, rhythmic breathing, deep bodywork. and intensive, highly confrontational group therapy. What made this combination so special were her special gifts. She had amazing intuition and a fearless ability to find your deepest pain, force her way in, and then be compassionately present with you. It was both extraordinarily healing and terrifying. Just as she'd promised, it helped me to release, then redirect, these passionate forces.

After my first private session with her, I felt freer and healthier. I'd already seen real results in people I knew but experiencing these positive results myself quickly made a believer out of me. I can still remember walking out of her office. That was the first time in my life when I absolutely knew that I could and would become someone that I myself would respect.

HEALING

Doris believed that the biggest part of healing was simply not hiding our pain, doubts, and fears. According to her, all forms of repression block our spirit from its true and natural expression. The therapy worked, but it was Doris herself who helped me to accept, appreciate, and love myself. I knew this was the real source of the healing I experienced, and over the next few years our relationship grew into much more than one of healer and patient. It became a true friendship with mutual respect.

As I began working with her to release my own spirit, I realized that healing was not all that Doris had to offer me. She was also very willing to train those who dedicated themselves to this work. This was her dream. She said that the true healing arts could not be learned from books. "To participate in the healing of another," she said, "is the great thrill and accomplishment of this life." Doris also facilitated her own experiences of letting go while working with several renowned Reichian therapists, including Fritz Perls and Israel Regardie. "There is no way you can know what another person is experiencing," she said, "but you can help if you are willing and able to let go of your own doubts, fears, and pain. To be a healer you must be experienced in letting go. It's like what a person experiences when they are falling in love. What we call 'falling' is the experience of letting go, and love is the great healer."

Six months after meeting Doris, she invited me, along with some of her most devoted students, to be her apprentice. There were about twelve of us who learned Doris' unique healing art, and this was the first step towards manifesting her vision of community. Doris had a vision of a new kind of community where people, especially children, were encouraged to trust and honor their instincts and feelings. Her unique therapy was designed to locate ingrained habitual patterns from childhood trauma, and then release them. With Doris' help, the twelve of us bought, remodeled, and lived communally in two mansions sitting side by side in the Hollywood Hills. Together we built a thriving jewelry company that made over $900,000 profit our first year in business (1974). Finally, we transformed a dingy old mental health clinic into Breakthrough Group Therapy Center, and the core of Doris' vision was complete.

The twelve of us all worked, ate, slept, learned, received, and practiced Doris' unique therapy together. Doris' inspiration originally came from Wilhelm Reich, but she was also an avid student of anything and everything that worked. We all studied Reich's books, The Function of the Orgasm, Discovery of the Orgone and The Murder of Christ, but Doris' healing art was uniquely her own. She was always on the lookout for talent, which she was wonderfully capable of nurturing. The positive changes and our rapidly growing list of clients at Breakthrough were testimonies to her methods of compassionate healing and hands-on instruction. I believe; however, her greatest accomplishment was in transforming her students, us, into such an effective and productive creative unit.

Like Doris, our amazing social experiment was bold and drew criticism from those who practiced the healing arts more conservatively. But, while they complained and criticized from their positions of authority, we were touching and helping many broken hearts and confused minds. During the four years I spent with Doris, every single day was an epic learning and growth experience. I loved the work and was good at it. For the first time in my life, I felt productive and like I belonged.

"We know what we are but know not what we may be."
William Shakespeare

REINVENTING MYSELF

Our mutual creative efforts, communal lifestyle, and active participation in one another's healing processes all made our family unique and very close. In every respect, what we had created together was more than any of us had ever imagined was possible. Nonetheless, I was ready to move on. After my prayer in Hawaii, I'd asked God to reveal my purpose here. From then on, I felt Him guiding me, and I always knew that my time with Doris was just to prepare me for something more. Just after Christmas, in January 1976, I packed my red '67 Camaro and headed east with only a vague idea of where I was going, or what I would do when I got there.

After the turmoil of the 60's, smuggling, nearly dying, and spending four incredibly intense years with Doris, I yearned for the ordinary. A heavy snowstorm forced me to stop and spend the night just outside Youngstown, Ohio. At breakfast the next morning, I had a long conversation with a young "Jesus freak" named Kathy. She was a "born again" Pentecostal seeking to recruit me into her church. There was really nowhere else to be, so I played along. As our conversation evolved, we discovered that we had something in common. We'd both escaped from, and defied the opinions of, our Catholic parents and the dominant authority of the church. As we talked, I saw Kathy's desire to recruit me, and I was overpowered by her desire to hear about my unique relationship with God. As we shared our stories and ideas, I was intrigued by her innocence and sincerity.

A few hours later, I drove on to Toledo, but all the way there I was thinking of our conversation. When I got to Toledo, I called her, and a couple of days later I returned to Youngstown to recruit Kathy as a lover and my first student. There were two major flaws to my plan. First, the roles of lover and teacher/healer are completely incompatible, and on that account alone our relationship was doomed. Kathy also was not interested in changing, but she went along to please me. That's not how it works, and we went around and round while we were both learning our lessons.

While living in Youngstown, I traveled, selling jewelry wholesale to small shops. It was really hard and not very profitable, so I decided to become an inventor. A year later, I was back in Los Angeles with a patent and an order from Sears. The buyer at the Sears home office in Chicago actually called a manufacturer in Dallas and asked if they would produce my first invention. As I was leaving his office with my prototype to sign the contracts in Dallas, the buyer grabbed my shoulder, looked deep into my eyes, and asked, "How often do you think this happens?" "Not too often," I replied. "Never," he said. "This never happens."

Back in California I bought the motorcycle I'd always wanted, and a few months later, on the Santa Monica Pier, I met Barbara, who became my wife. I visited with Doris occasionally, but that part of my life was over. Being in love melted everything else away, and suddenly it was 1982. Barb and I had been together five years, and we already had four young children. I had developed several more patents and was president of my own corporation, "Progressive Fitness, Inc." We'd just landed our first order for my newest invention, "The Total Trainer," and it was already in production. I felt confident that the gobs of money we were about to make would help compensate for my shortcomings as a parent and husband.

After three long years of negotiating, investing, staying up long nights, and risking all our money, I was flying high. We were finally that close, but in just a few hours my dream came tumbling down. The manufacturer's representative, who was taking all our orders, had a death in his immediate family. Devastated and unable to work, he backed out of our deal. That would have been fine, but some of our investors and partners sued us for breach of contract. There was no such contract, but in the U.S., anyone can sue anyone for anything. It was just as if Captain Hook had raided my Never Land, and we couldn't afford the fight. They forced me out, and that was that!

In just one day, all our savings and hopes of a secure financial future were gone. As my parents and teachers all predicted, I was officially a failure. Suddenly, old friends were calling to share their own thriving, yet conservative careers. It seemed as if everyone and everything was trying to remind me that refusing to grow up or buckle down was the mistake of a lifetime. In truth, I hadn't refused, I just couldn't. Now, though, my family would suffer for my irresponsible choices, and I was certain that they would all be better off without me.

WHAT DO YOU WANT?

It was just before Christmas in 1982. I couldn't find a job, and I had plenty of time to think and wonder about what had happened. For the first seven years after my prayer in Hawaii, I felt myself being prepared for something. I was certain then that my life would serve God and my fellow man in some special way. Now all I could think about was what were we going to do about

Christmas? It was late in the afternoon. I was still in my PJ's. Feeling especially depressed and exhausted, I collapsed on our bed. Then I started praying for the first time in years, but soon fell asleep. When I awoke, it was evening. Our room was dark except for a beam of light that illuminated just one small book in our bookcase.

I couldn't see where that light was coming from, so I went to the bookcase and pulled out the little book. Buckminister Fuller, a visionary and award-winning architect, was the author. "Bucky," as he was affectionately known, was concerned with the issues of pollution and conservation long before anyone else. He had proclaimed that conservation was vital to our existence on Spaceship Earth, and he was laughed at and ridiculed for doing so. However, Bucky was a true believer and a pioneer. While reading his words, I began to wonder about my own passions. I remembered being very passionate when I was younger, but now I felt so empty.

In his book, Bucky described how his brilliant career began when he was thirty-two, a year younger than me at the time. Like me, he was bankrupt and out of work. He'd seen his beloved young daughter, Alexandra, die of complications from polio and spinal meningitis. I had to be thankful; at least our children were all in good health. Also, like me, Bucky felt ineffective, and believed that his family would be better off without him. He even felt suicidal; but, as he was about to end his life, a voice within him suggested, "Before ending your life, you might try living it."

"Perhaps there are some things you would like to do before your life is over," the voice said. Then Bucky realized how his life was spent struggling to do what others said he *should* do. "Living to please others was not really living," he thought. Reading this, I realized that in my own struggle for freedom, I was also not really living my true life. I was consumed with resisting and rebelling against what "they" expected of me. In that respect, Bucky and I were opposites, but our results were the same. By allowing our choices to be defined by other peoples' expectations, we both were unconscious of what we truly wanted.

> *"I set about fifty-five years ago (1927) to see what a penniless, unknown human individual with a dependent wife and newborn child might be able to do effectively on behalf of all humanity..."*   Buckminister Fuller

As I was realizing this, I, too, heard a voice within me. It was asking, "So, what do you want?" All I could think of was, "I just want to be a good father." "So," the voice asked, "what did you want from your father?" My answer was clear: "Permission to have a dream and to be myself." "And how could your father have given that to you?" the voice asked. I had to think for a moment. "By his example," I said, and there was a long silence. Finally, I saw that, to be a good father, I must set a good example by following my own heart.

Once I realized this, my voice asked again, "So what do you want?" Then all I could think of was "money," but the voice stopped me. "If you had all the money and every other thing that you might need, what would you do?" Of course, I'd dreamt of having such freedom, but I never actually thought of what I would do with it. I felt stuck until the voice asked, "When do you remember feeling most alive?" A stream of happy and

34

exciting moments flowed through me, until my mind finally came to rest. I saw myself, seven years old and kneeling. My heart full of hope, I was saying, "Our Father who art in heaven, hallowed be thy name...."

I realized that I hadn't even thought of the Lord's Prayer since I was a child. Then I remembered my parents' fight and why I'd abandoned my faith and that prayer. I also realized how it had inspired me and how, since that night, I felt that something was missing. For twenty-six years I'd been trying to fill the empty place that the prayer had once filled, and that's what I wanted. I wanted to feel that alive and hopeful again. I also realized that my seven-year-old inner child had been waiting right where I left him twenty-six years earlier. He still believed in the promise of that prayer, so what did I have to lose? Right then I rejoined his quest to know the magical potential of the Lord's Prayer, and this simple intent has now filled me with life and hope for twenty-five years.

BORN AGAIN

After this experience, I was compelled to read just a bit more of Bucky's little book. I learned that, when he began living his new life, he pursued only what he was truly interested in. He discovered that anyone, with just fifteen hours of research, could become an expert in anything. They would then have more information about the subject than 95% of other people. Bucky also said that the most innovative thinkers are self-taught and pursue their interests, not as professionals, but as passionate individuals.

The tricks to a new beginning, he advised, are first to begin, then to choose and devote yourself to your most passionate interests, regardless of public opinion or issues of practicality. Nearly everything Bucky said seemed to have been written just for me. With his encouraging words and my newly reclaimed passion for the Lord's Prayer, I set out to become an expert on that prayer. The moment I made this decision, however, a chorus of critical and discouraging voices rose up within me. "Are you nuts?" "Who do you think you are?" "Praying won't pay the rent." And on and on they went, but I knew these voices. They were the ones that led me to that dark and empty place. So, I stood up to them. I told them that they could talk all they wanted, but I had a new voice to listen to, my own.

Now I'm going to ask Barbara to share what happened next.

BARBARA: When I saw Bodie after he'd had this experience, I was so relieved to see that the dark cloud had lifted from him. Until then, I really wasn't sure if our relationship would survive. He told me what had happened, and I was overjoyed. When I was a child, I had also experienced something magical while the congregation of our church said the Lord's Prayer. I asked Bodie to say it with me. As we prayed together, for the first time since I was a child, I remembered the wondrous expectations I'd felt while saying this prayer.

Like Bodie, I'd felt that I was the only one having this experience. I, too, doubted myself and gradually abandoned my faith. Hearing Bodie's story and praying with him that evening transported me back to that earlier time. Once more, I felt my own precious experience of hope and faith while saying the Lord's Prayer in the little red church I'd attended. Praying together felt so good, that I asked if we could say it again and again. As we prayed, the stresses that had been pushing us further apart were replaced with a new bond. Since then, while we have certainly faced many challenges, we have faced them together.

After our union that evening, our life together began fresh and new. The next day, Bodie found a rare, leather-bound book titled The Lord's Prayer. He was led right to it, and we both saw this book as a confirmation of Spirit supporting our new quest. Ralph M. De Bit wrote the book in 1924. He was a self-proclaimed metaphysician, an occultist dedicated to "the sacred science". Though his thoughts and words boggled our minds, they also encouraged our hearts; and this is what we needed most at the beginning of our long journey ahead.

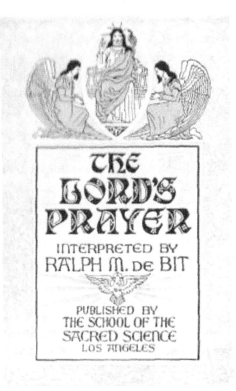

I have to laugh here, as it's taken us twenty-five years to understand what Mr. De Bit was saying in 1924. Our path was different from his. We've not approached this prayer with our intellects, but as children. We both sincerely believed in its magical promise long before we understood it. Our efforts have brought us to many of the same conclusions that Mr. De Bit expressed in his book, and our journey together has been wondrous. We celebrate daily how this prayer that Jesus taught has blessed our lives, as well as the blossoming lives of our children and grandchildren, and the hundreds of people with whom we have shared our discoveries.

THE LORD'S PRAYER

SPIRITUAL (Atma)	Our Father, which art in Heaven. Thy will be done.	Will—Atma.
INTUITIONAL (Buddhi)	Thy Kingdom come.	Kingdom—Buddhi.
CAUSAL (Abstract Mental or Manas)	Hallowed be Thy Name.	Name—Manas.
CONCRETE MENTAL (Intellect)	Deliver us from Evil.	Evil—Intellect.
ASTRAL (Desire Body)	Lead us not into Temptation.	Temptation—Desire.
PHYSICAL { Etheric	Forgive us our Debts as we forgive our Debtors.	
Dense	Give us this day our Daily Bread.	

Son of God

Divine Man and His Image

Son of Man

(CHART FROM DE BIT BOOK)

BODIE: Mr. De Bit inspired us with thoughts like these:

"It is within the simple spiritual facts dealt with in this simple prayer that the deepest occult truths lie concealed. To search for these truths with an unbiased mind leads to an understanding, which enables the earnest student to see how full of wisdom and power are the mysterious links which bind together the spiritual life of humanity."

And these:

38

"When man can understand and practice meditation, he can, by being absorbed therein, merge himself in spirit with the Divine Spiritual currents flowing through the universe. Even when one does not understand meditation, one can receive great benefit by dwelling in thought on one or the other of the formulae, which have originated with the great Spiritual leaders of mankind. Such a thought is a living force and is always sustained by the power and inspiration of the consciousness of the Spiritual Elder Brother who first gave expression to it. Anyone meditating in this simple way and letting the formula live in his consciousness, will, imperceptibly, begin to live in the current of higher spirituality. A power will stream through him of which he will steadily grow more and more conscious. If he has the patience to persevere until the power flows into him in a sufficient measure, he will experience increased physical energy, a cleaner emotional time, indicated by more spontaneous enjoyment of wholesome pleasure, and a keener alertness and joy in the pursuit of knowledge. This increased physical, moral and intellectual strength will in time be followed by an awakening of those latent spiritual faculties and powers, which are the heritage of every Ego."

When I saw this small book in the used bookstore, hidden amongst dozens of dusty old Bibles, I knew I was guided to it. I was already dwelling in thought on the Lord's Prayer. The child in me had always seen it as the formula, which originated with Jesus and knowing that others saw the Lord's Prayer as I did it made all the difference.

"Give me the children until they are seven and anyone may have them afterward".   Saint Frances Xavier

Today, my eye occasionally falls on that little book sitting on my desk. It was written over eighty years ago, and it still encourages me. It's not the book's content, but the miracle of finding it, which inspires me. It's been twenty-six years, and I am as appreciative of this encouragement now as I was then. Sometimes my heart still skips a beat, as it reminds me of how Spirit supports us in discovering what the Lord's Prayer promises.

Part II
"BE HERE NOW"

TOWER OF BABBLE BY GUSTAVE DORE

RIDDLES IN TIME

Since Barbara and I both strayed from our religions when we were quite young and later gravitated towards Eastern spiritual practices, neither of us were versed on the teachings of the Bible. As we began pursuing our childhood instincts concerning the magical promise of the Lord's Prayer, we were not sure where to begin.

First, we went to where Jesus first taught the Lord's Prayer in his Sermon on the Mount. There we found what we thought were three riddles with which Jesus prepares us to receive his prayer. Then we went to the very beginning of his ministry, to the very first thing that he taught. As you will see, the insights that we gained from these beginnings, together with our knowledge of Eastern religions and the encouragement we received from Mr. De Bit's book all enabled us to see the Lord's Prayer in a whole new way.

In Matthew 6: 5-13, during the Sermon on the Mount, Jesus said, *"When you pray, enter into your closet, and when you have closed the door, pray to your Father who sees in secret and he will reward you openly."* This is the first riddle, and the *closet* Jesus speaks of reminded us of an inner place known to those who meditate as the "seat of the soul." It's located in the center of your head slightly above your eyes in the area of the brain called the pineal gland. Take a moment and move your attention there, and you may feel an opening. This is the *closet* that we *enter* and *close the door* (our eyes) to *"Love God with all your heart and with all our soul and with all our mind"* (Matthew 22: 36-40). By doing this, we *"Seek the kingdom of God within us,"* (Luke 17: 21). This just made sense to us.

Then we saw the obvious connection between the words *"Hallowed be thy name"* in the Lord's Prayer, and Mantra Yoga that we had been practicing for years. Mantra Yoga is a way of knowing God intimately by worshiping His Holy Name (*Hallowed be Thy Name*). One does this by chanting sacred names while focusing attention on the pineal area of the brain. It occurred to us that the Lord's Prayer might be a form of Mantra Yoga.

The two riddles, which precede the prayer also confirm this. We will explain these riddles in Parts III & IV.

THE ULTIMATE TROJAN HORSE

When Barbara and I were children, we lost faith in our churches because the promise we felt was contradicted by threats and judgments. The promise was illusive, but the threat was clear. We are all born sinners and given this one short life to *repent* our evil ways or go to hell. We were too young to realize the absurdity of thinking that Jesus would say this. We were also too inexperienced to appreciate the beautiful promise that these same words express. We believe that by allowing for this common misunderstanding, Jesus gave the arrogant "might makes right" paradigm the ultimate verbal "Trojan Horse."

In Matthew 5:17, we learn that, after his 40 days and nights in the desert, *"Jesus began to preach and to say, 'Repent for the kingdom of God is at hand.'"* This is the first thing Jesus taught, so everything that follows is intended to embellish this first simple message. The priests and ministers of our churches expressed his first teaching to emphasize our sinful nature and the threat of damnation. But can you hear Jesus making such threats? *You sinners better clean up your acts before your short, miserable lives are over, or you will burn forever in hell.* Or does this next promise sound more like him? *Stop looking here and there for God's kingdom. It is in the here and now. It is within you. Repent for the kingdom of God is at hand* may be interpreted either way. It's up to us to decide which rings true.

BE HERE NOW

In Matthew 18:3 Jesus said, *"Except ye be converted, and become as little children, ye shall not enter into the kingdom of heaven."* Children naturally live in the present, where God is. Buckminster Fuller and many other wise souls have embraced the motto *less is more.* In the old "might makes right" paradigm, this sounds absurd, but by letting go, we enter the heavenly present where *all these things (our needs) shall be added unto us.* That's the promise of the Lord's Prayer, designed for us to realize in our own unique way.

I was seeing it this way for the first time, and I wondered if everything Jesus taught was about *the kingdom of God is at hand.* Then I remembered a book by Baba Ram Dass called *Be Here Now.* In my earlier period of hippie/surfer/smuggler, I was a fan of Richard Alpert before he became Baba Ram Dass. While on the faculty at Harvard, he collaborated with Timothy Leary, Ralph Metzner, Aldous Huxley, Allen Ginsberg, and others doing extensive research with LSD and other psychedelic chemicals. In 1967 Richard changed in India when he met an enlightened Yogi master. Neem Karoli Baba introduced Richard Alpert to meditation and gave him his new name, Ram Dass, which means "servant of God."

As we both came to God by way of LSD, and because his book *Be Here Now* gave me my first practical experience and understanding of meditation, Yoga, and Eastern spirituality, I always felt close to Ram Dass. Realizing that *Be Here Now* is also what Jesus taught helped me to see how many times I'd received lessons in being present. Remembering events stretching over the whole course of my life, I realized how different my life would have been had I not answered each of those calls to be here now. Being spiritual was, above all, just about being present.

A MIRACLE

One very dark night in the summer of 1969, I was driving between Tijuana and Tecate with 250 kilos of Mexican grass in the trunk of my car, when I came face to face with the promise. Rounding the bend of a rough Mexican country road, I saw flashing lights, and my heart nearly stopped. It was a new roadblock, and the sight of it released a stampede of thoughts trampling my mind. There was nothing I could do. As if this wasn't scary enough, earlier that week some friends and I had visited a mutual friend, Ray, who was serving a fifteen-year sentence in Mesa Prison. Ray had been caught in a roadblock with 27 kilos on that very same road.

Like me, Ray was driving kilos from Tijuana to a farm outside Tecate, where backpackers would walk them through a deep canyon beyond the reach of the border patrol's radar. Now he was in Mesa Prison, which was run by gangs who bought and sold the other prisoners as slaves. The whole time we were there, this tough guy was trembling, crying, and begging us to get him out. He was certain that it wasn't a matter of whether he would be raped, tortured, and or murdered, but when.

Now, on that country road, there were just two cars between me, that checkpoint, and quite possibly Mesa Prison. Soon the Federales, opening the trunk of the car ahead of me, would be looking into my eyes. It didn't really matter that the weight of the kilos had my bumper practically dragging on the ground, and in my back seat were fourteen backpacks and the spare tire. Maybe I could tell him I was helping a bunch of Boy Scouts to earn their Hike Baja Merit Badges! Then the car in front of me drove off, and the stampeding thoughts stopped. I felt completely calm.

As my car rolled up to the checkpoint, everything was moving in slow motion. The Federales bent down, but before he could look into my eyes or the back seat, something happened. He glanced toward his partner, stood up, and started speaking really fast. Without looking back at me, he just waved me through. I didn't believe in God or heaven, but I knew something more than luck had just saved me. Later that night, after evading two United States helicopters, I discovered that the people I was working for knew about that roadblock and hadn't told me. Two weeks later, Channel 10 News filmed the police raiding their million-dollar home. They went to jail and I went to Hawaii.

ENLIGHTENMENT

There have been many extreme events that compelled me to be present. I saw that after each of these, my life changed for the better. It had seemed to me and everyone else that my life had no purpose or direction, but all along God was calling and guiding me to be with Him/Her in the present. There were other memories and other lessons. One evening, as I was praying with the intention to be present, I remembered being a child again. I was in church with my mother, and she was telling me, *"This is God's house."* I believed her, and I could feel God's presence there, but was God more present in that church? No. But because I believed He was, naturally I was more present in his house and therefore more aware of Him.

This idea that Jesus was simply teaching and encouraging people to "be here now" made sense. That's what all spiritual teachers do, and in this light many of his most enigmatic thoughts became clear. Jesus said, for example, *"The light of the body is the eye: if therefore you let your eye be single, your whole body shall be full of light."* (Matt.6:23) This is exactly how the Eastern Yogis describe "enlightenment". Thinking of the Lord's Prayer as a Yoga exercise that teaches us to achieve "enlightenment" through relaxing into the present also made sense. This point of view enabled us to see how this prayer is beautifully expressed on multiple levels at once. For example, *Give us this day our daily bread* isn't just a physical request for enough to eat, and *Forgive us our trespasses as we forgive those who trespass against us* isn't solely about our emotional need to relieve our conscience. Both also fulfill our highest spiritual need to enter the present and transcend the illusion that we are separate from God and each other.

Seeing every part of the Lord's Prayer as an exercise for coming into the present did more than make perfect sense, it also worked. It was just as Mr. De Bit had described in his little book: *"Anyone meditating in this simple way and letting the formula live in his consciousness, will, imperceptibly, begin to live in the current of higher spirituality. A power will stream through him of which he will steadily grow more and more conscious."* What he was describing was just what it feels like to be fully present.

BREATHING

Once I'd forgotten about the promise of the Lord's Prayer, I said it by memory, as most people do. I could say it very quickly while thinking of something else entirely. That's what Jesus called vain repetition. It's a waste of time to say or do anything without feeling it, especially something imbued with such promise. Seeing a similarity between what Jesus taught and what the Eastern Yogis taught encouraged us to try using various techniques we were taught while learning to meditate. One of these was rhythmic breathing.

The importance of breathing properly while meditating is common knowledge. To meditate, practice Yoga, or do any form of exercise, for that matter, proper breathing is essential. Breathing is the one thing that we all do both consciously and subconsciously. This is why breathing consciously is so relaxing, as it unifies the two hemispheres of our brain. The importance of uniting our conscious thinking mind and our subconscious feeling inner child is well known to any serious practitioner of Yoga or meditation.

Practically speaking, Yoga breathing strengthens our respiratory and immune systems. Breathing consciously reduces stress, is energizing, and produces greater alertness, both physically and mentally. Meditating on our breathing also helps promote physical, emotional, and mental healing. Anapana sati is a meditation on the in-and-out rhythms of our breathing that Buddha taught, and we believe Jesus likely taught it, as well. There are natural rhythms within the Lord's Prayer and breathing as we pray helps to savor and personalize your prayer. You can easily feel this for yourself right now.

- **Our** (in breath) **Father** (out breath)
- **Who art** (in) **In Heaven** (out)
- **Hallowed be** (in) **Thy name** (out)

Do this a few times and see how it helps you to relax and focus on each word. In Part VII you will have numerous opportunities to breathe and pray this way.

THE CHAKRAS

One morning, while breathing my way through the Lord's Prayer, I had an interesting thought. Since childhood, I've been fascinated with numbers; and it occurred to me that the Bible speaks of the Seven Heavens, the seven sisters who found Moses in the desert, the seven churches, seven candlesticks, and the seven spirits of God. The Lord's Prayer also has seven segments. Then I remembered a Yoga exercise of breathing through the seven chakras in our bodies (see the image). Naturally, I

wondered if there was a connection between these seven energy centers and the seven segments of the Lord's Prayer.

For those who are not familiar with the chakras or energy centers, the Yogi masters of the Far East teach that they correlate to the major nerve ganglia branching forth from our spinal column. They say that each chakra correlates to a specific level of consciousness, a developmental stage of life, a color, a sound, and a bodily function. Many of the spiritual exercises they teach are specifically designed to align, open, or activate these chakras. They compare our bodies to an engine or computer that must be properly wired and maintained to operate at its full potential.

Once this thought came to mind, it didn't take long to see that there is indeed a correlation between these chakras and the seven segments of the Lord's Prayer. You may easily confirm this for yourself by contemplating how each part of the prayer relates to the corresponding parts of your own body as show in the previous image.

YOGA

Our discoveries of the Lord's Prayer were deeply influenced by our years of experience with Mantra Yoga. We knew that this form of Yoga was very old and part of many ancient religions. We also saw how the core philosophy behind this form of Yoga was present within the Lord's Prayer (*Hallowed be Thy name*). Encouraged by these insights, the prayer's breathing rhythms, and its obvious connection to the chakras, we continued looking to the East for more insights into this prayer. We learned that Yoga is at least 5,500 years old; and, as with Christianity, there are hundreds of different kinds of Yoga. Originally, however, all these expressions of Yoga came from seven roots or branches.

There it was again, the number seven! It didn't take us long to see how all seven of these original branches of Yoga were also present within the Lord's Prayer. You may observe these correlations in the image on the previous page. So as not to interfere with the flow of our story, we have reserved our deeper explanations of these connections and exercises for Part VII, where you may actually experience them.

THE HIDDEN TRUTH

How could this have gone unnoticed for so long? Had Jesus intentionally hidden these insights? Did he plan to keep them secret until the information age would enable us to see them; and if so, why now? For that matter, why us? Or was this just a testimony to how all enlightened souls see the same truth but express it differently, according to the needs and traditions of their times and places? We won't find the answers to any of the questions in history books. There are no experts or authorities to ask. So, each of us must rely on our own experiences to prove or disprove our own questions. This too is perfect, as the only way to know the truth is to find it within ourselves.

SHAPING MOTIVATION

BARBARA: During this early stage, as we were developing our new understanding of Jesus and his prayer, important insights seemed to be coming from practically everyone and everything that we encountered. Once we made our commitment to know the magic of the prayer Jesus taught, everything and everyone in our lives seemed to be dedicated to helping us.

One evening Bodie and I watched a televised interview with the Dalai Lama. When we heard how this amazing man begins each day at 3:00 am and spends his first six hours every day engaged in various meditations, with both spiritual and mental exercises, we were both deeply impressed. The interviewer, however, was obviously bewildered by this, and he asked the Dalai Lama what he hoped to accomplish in those first six hours of each day. A gentle smile brightened the Dalai Lama's face. He seemed very pleased by this question as he paused and thoughtfully replied, "*Shaping motivation.*"

Hearing his answer, Bodie and I turned to each other and smiled too. The Dalai Lama's answer was the most wonderful affirmation of what we'd been learning about the Lord's Prayer. Shaping motivation is refining our own understanding of what we really want, so we can focus on that and that alone. We are creators; what motivates us also defines what we manifest. The Dalai Lama spends those six hours every morning to ensure that the rest of his day will be spent manifesting what he truly wants to accomplish. This is also what the Lord's Prayer does. You could even say that Jesus created his prayer specifically for shaping motivation.

BODIE: For years, in order to have the time that I needed to pursue my real interests, I worked nights as a waiter in the nicest country clubs and fine restaurants. I made good money, but I always hated it. It enabled me to pursue my dreams of success, but, as I've shared with you, those dreams were not what I truly wanted.

That fateful night in 1982, after reclaiming my passion for the Lord's Prayer, I wondered how I would find the time to pursue this renewed passion. I quickly thought of getting a job as waiter and was immediately surprised. It wasn't surprising that I thought of it, but rather that I was not repulsed by this thought, as I had been so many times in the past. I immediately saw that a time would come when I would want to share this passion with others, and I saw that waiting tables was an excellent way of honing the people skills I would need to do this.

Unlike my past experiences, I found a good job easily. Before that, I'd never kept a job for much more than a year. Miraculously, this time I kept the job for seven years. What had been pure drudgery became a truly joyous experience for me. I was, and still am, deeply grateful for that job. I believe that the transformation that made this possible is a result of what the Dalai Lama calls shaping motivation. Knowing what we really want and experiencing how the whole world is helping us to get it is the magic that Jesus described when he said, *"Seek first the kingdom of God and all these things shall be added unto you."*

BUDDHA

BODIE: When I was nine years old, our family went to San Francisco on vacation. On our first night there, we ate at a nice Chinese restaurant in Chinatown. After dinner, we took a walk and looked in the windows of the shops nearby. In one of those windows, I saw the most fantastic dagger. It had a gleaming curved blade and a deep blue and gold cloisonné handle and sheath. It captivated my active imagination, and I could not move from that window until my parents promised that we would return the next day when the shop was open.

My mother didn't want me to have a dagger, but surprisingly she did not protest. The next day my heart sank when I learned that the dagger cost $56. I had managed to save only $15, though, at $1 per lawn, that was a lot to me. Seeing my disappointment, the Chinese shopkeeper asked me, "Do you know Buddha?" I didn't know who or what Buddha was, so he told me a story about Buddha, and I left his shop that day proudly holding my new two-foot-high golden ceramic Buddha.

For the next nine years, his peaceful, smiling countenance sat in the center of my dresser. He looked over me as I slept, he was there to greet me when I awoke, and he was still there when I came home from school. Though I never thought much about him, he was always there. As I began developing my new relationship with Jesus through his prayer, I realized how similar he and Buddha really were.

THE NARROW GATE

Jesus said the way to heaven is *the straight and narrow gate*, and Buddha described the way to Nirvana as *the middle path*. I now believe they were both simply describing how to be present. Buddha taught the art of perfect detachment, and Jesus taught the art of perfect engagement. These two are opposites, but both lead to the present where there are no opposites or opposition. In the present, we are like babes nursing, just as God made us. Jesus instructed, *"Be perfect, even as your Father which is in heaven is perfect" (Matthew 5:48)*. I used to think this was impossible. If I couldn't live up to the standards set forth by my parents, teachers, the church, and society in general, how could I ever hope to be perfect? As with all of His riddles, the answer to this one is simple. What makes God perfect is that He/She is God. In this riddle, Jesus emphasized that being perfect is the same for us. He's not telling us to be like God, but to be true to ourselves.

In describing the narrow gate of perfection, Jesus tells us, *"It is easier for a camel to go through the eye of the needle, than for a rich man to enter into the kingdom of God"* (Matthew 19: 24). Again, this riddle sounds impossible to understand, and even more impossible to do. In truth, the eye of the needle was a narrow gate within the main gate of ancient Jerusalem. When a caravan arrived after sundown, the larger gate was already closed to protect against nocturnal attacks. Therefore, the camels of the caravan had to be unloaded and then crawl through the needle on their knees. If, and when, you experience the Lord's Prayer as we do, you will see how the prayer Jesus taught helps to unload our worldly burdens in order to enter the present—humbly, on our knees in prayer.

SOLOMON'S REQUEST

As I pray, I experience the shaping of my motivation much like the shaping of a gemstone. In the beginning, it just looks like an ordinary rock; but, gradually, chipping exposes its crystalline heart. When the chipping is over, the polishing of the crystal begins. Only after it is shaped so that it catches and reflects the light in the most advantageous way possible is it complete. Shaping human motivation is very similar, but as long as we are here on earth, the shaping goes on and on. We are not complete until the dance of our lives is over, because the great illusions that distract us from the present are ever changing.

There is a beautiful Old Testament story about the gem within us all that shines with God's light when we are living in the present. It's what I experienced, praying with all my heart, when I was seven. It's what we all experience when we are falling in love, and the freedom that we all seek is to live in that blessed state without any reason at all. What I am talking about is the key that always and everywhere unlocks *the kingdom of God at hand*. It is the heart of the story about how young King Solomon became the wisest, wealthiest, and most powerful king on earth.

"In Givon, the Lord appeared to Solomon in a dream by night. And God said, ask what shall I grant you. And Solomon said, You have shown great faithful love to your servant David, my father, because he walked before You in Faithfulness and in integrity of heart. And You have kept for him this great faithful love, by giving him a

son to sit on his throne, as it is this day. And now, O Lord, my God, You have made Your servant king in place of my father David, yet I am but a lad...........Give, then, Your servant a listening heart to judge Your people, to distinguish between good and evil; for who can judge this vast people of yours?" (I Kings 3:5-9)

King Solomon could have asked God for anything and received it, but he asked for a listening heart, and this is also what a true prayer develops.

"And God was pleased that Solomon had asked for this. And God said to him, Because you have asked for this thing, and did not ask for long life, nor have you asked for riches, nor have you asked for the life of your enemies, but have asked for discernment to listen in judgment, behold, I have done as you have spoken. I have given you a heart that is wise and understanding; so that there has never been anyone like you before, nor shall anyone like you arise again. And I will also give you that which you have not asked for, both riches and glory, all your life, the like of which no king has ever had." (1 Kings 3:10-13)

It was a listening heart that enabled young King Solomon to receive the greatest wealth, power, and glory that any earthly king has ever known. A listening heart is an open one. It is an empty heart. In Psalm. 109: 22, God says, *"My heart is empty within me."* This is how we come into the present to receive God's gift of Himself, and this is what the Lord's Prayer does. It empties our heart so that we may listen to receive, as young King Solomon did.

"And God gave Solomon wisdom and great understanding, and a heart as broad as the sand upon the seashore" (1 Kings 4:29).

A gift freely given, no matter how precious, may also be taken for granted and forgotten. Later in his life, King Solomon obviously did forget. If he had developed his listening heart with the Lord's Prayer, perhaps he could have passed his great treasure forward to future generations. Imagine a world with everyone listening from his or her hearts. That's the promise!

(KING SOLOMON)

Part III
The Dance Within

SOMETHING SPECIAL

I've just described how our knowledge of Eastern religions and spiritual practices has enabled us to see how the promise of the Lord's Prayer is available to us all in the here and now. This foundational understanding was revealed through common knowledge about Yoga and meditation. Now, in Part III, I will describe how my distinctive education in the field of psychology, along with our creative imaginations, has enabled us to build upon this foundation in a very special way. Then, in Part IV, we start to see and experience how the prayer Jesus taught was also revealed to us in much more exiting, fun, personal, and challenging ways.

THE SECOND RIDDLE

Proverbs 23:7 states, *"As you think, in your heart you shall become,"* clearly emphasizing what every psychologist and spiritual student knows. What we think profoundly affects not only how we feel, but also what we create. By changing how we think, we shape our motives to change what we experience, altering our whole reality. The second riddle, or key, with which Jesus prepares us to receive His prayer, is this: *"But when you pray, do not use vain repetitions as the heathen do."* In other words, pray with feeling or pray from your heart. Reciting this prayer from memory without thinking or feeling is *vain repetition.* It is vain because it changes nothing. The primary key to experiencing the Lord's Prayer as an effective transcendental spiritual tool is to think and feel with every breath and word. Do you see how breathing and focusing on the chakras as you pray can help you to feel this prayer? Try it now.

As you practice praying this way, you will quickly realize how that feeling the words of the Lord's Prayer is really very easy. In the years that I spent working with Doris August, I experienced Transactional Analysis, which teaches that there are three primary ego-states. These are the Parent, Adult, and Child, whose interactions define us. Each of these three inner selves has its own language and function. The Parent's language is one of values, the rational Adult's language is of logic and intellect, and the Child's language is of feeling, emotion, intuition, and pure creativity. To pray, experience, or live our highest and truest potential, all of these aspects must be as one. I believe this is what Jesus meant when he said, *"Let your eye be single and your whole body shall be filled with light."*

When Barbara and I were children, our innocent Child hearts felt the promise of the Lord's Prayer before our inner Adults were sufficiently developed to support our feelings with understanding. Our inner Parents were not yet ready to guide or protect us; so, by default, the beliefs of our earthly parents, teachers, and churches defined our realities. Few of us have grown up in a world where our childhood feelings were supported or understood. Therefore, by the time most of us are adults, our inner child has retreated into seclusion, and/or is in a state of rebellion. The combination of these two is called passive aggressive behavior, which is a product of our excessively mental, adult society.

The nature of a child is the same as The Promise. Children live in the present. It is true that, as *we think in our hearts, we shall become,* but to be happy we must *follow our bliss* into *God's Kingdom at hand.* In our very adult world, however, that's just not practical, is it? Today, children are being prepared and trained almost from birth to become efficient, productive, hard-working adults. This makes sense until we realize The Promise. Is the way to be happy too simple for our adult mind to accept? Can we guide our heart to where it really wants to be? That's what the Lord's Prayer is designed to help us do.

CREATING THE CHARACTERS

As Barbara & I were developing our new relationships with Jesus and the Lord's Prayer, we naturally wanted to share it with our children. With this in mind, I began telling them bedtime stories. I created a new character in each story, and right away it was clear that the kids were more interested in these characters than in my stories. They asked, "What do they look like?", "What powers do they have?", "Who are their friends and enemies?", etc. Now that I think about it, I'm not really sure if they were that interested, or if that was just a clever way of distracting me and postponing the inevitable "lights out".

(LUVVINS IN SCHOOL)

Their favorites characters, and ours, were the "Luvvins." "Everybody needs a little luvvin." These Luvvins had heart-shaped bodies, and ears that were also wings. When there was a problem, the Luvvins would call upon "The Power of Love" (Our Creator) to defeat "The Enemies of Love", the "Fearies, Greedies, Guilties"; and the ultimate villain, "Sleeze". When I'd created a full cast of sixteen characters, the adult inventor/entrepreneur in me saw a business opportunity.

We hired Lane Reichart, a superb young animation artist who worked for Hanna Barbera. Lane agreed to take on this side work because he was buying his first house and needed some extra money. Soon, however, he was also seeing how special these characters were. "They seem so eager to be seen," he said, and this was also what I'd experienced

when I first conjured them up. What amazed Lane even more, however, was that, with no experience in that business, I was able to take his drawings to Steve Waterman, the best animation agent in the business, and got him to represent us. Apparently, Lane had been trying unsuccessfully to get Steve to represent him for quite some time.

Steve quickly stirred up interest with some big toy companies and animation studios, including Hanna Barbera. The characters and I were taking meetings all over town, and again visions of wealth were dancing in my head. Finally, however, a series of sobering disappointments brought me down to earth, back to the Lord's Prayer. As I was letting go of my Hollywood dreams, I felt some disappointment, but I was also relieved. While reflecting on how experiencing our characters as a business had temporarily suspended my delight in pursuing The Promise, I had an interesting thought: "What if there was a relationship between our sixteen characters, the chakras, and the Lord's Prayer?"

LUVVINS AND A GREEDIE

A VISION

At first, it seemed like a long shot, but this question kept bouncing around in my head; until one morning in the shower, I saw it. Before the hot water ran out, I was seeing two characters per chakra, one positive and one negative, and understanding how these inner relationships define us. I saw the Lord's Prayer healing our hearts and minds by uniting these characteristics, thus transforming our mundane, conflicting inner selves into one wondrous Spirit-guided, and intricately meshed bio-energetic mechanism. First I felt it, then I saw it, ebbing and flowing with positive and negative currents swirling together the way warm and cool air unite in a storm. I looked into the eye of this storm and heard, "*Focus on the dance, not the dancers.*" I understood this to mean *let our eye be single* and *our whole body shall be filled with light.* I saw this inner dance uniting the opposites within us and the result of this way of "dancing" was enlightenment.

Finally, as I was drying off after that amazing shower, I instantly saw how our sixteen characters, the chakras, and the prayer could be crafted into a new kind of game. By the time I had finished, I saw how this new game would teach us to use our unique life webs the way a spider does, to attract *all these things* and to experience these things *being added unto us.*

My spiritual studies and experiences with psychology, macrobiotics, and even psychedelic drugs had all prepared me to receive this vision. Most of all it reminded me of Doris. For the first time, I was certain that what I had absorbed during the thousands of hours I'd spent with Doris would be very useful. The last time I'd seen her, in the hospital just before she died, it was obvious that Doris was still trying to understand what had happened between us. We had both been so certain that I would follow in her footsteps. Now, I could see her smiling and understanding what I was seeing, and feeling better than I did, myself.

The key was just as Doris always said; it was all about surrendering to the moment. This is also what the Lord's Prayer is all about. Like the prayer from which it came, I knew this new game would help to mend the divisions between our own inner selves by uniting them in this dance with Our Father. I didn't know how this could happen in a game, but I was certain that this was what I was seeing and feeling.

CREATING THE GAME

As I set out to create this game, my experiences with "games" such as the I Ching, Tarot, and Runes were helpful. Like them, our new game would use the principles of synchronicity (random selection, i.e. rolling dice). I knew that Christians generally look down on such mystical games, but I found affirming references to this method of selection and guidance right in the Bible. In Acts 1:15-26, Judas Iscariot's successor as an apostle was selected by throwing lots. Proverbs 16:33 reveals, *"The lot is cast into the lap: but the whole decision is of the Lord."* I also learned how the ancient Hebrew Priesthood used mysterious oracular devices, called the Urim and Thummim, to consult with God. Urim is derived from the Hebrew for "light", or "to give light"; and Thummin means "completeness", "perfection", or "innocence". (Ex. 28:30, Lv. 8:8, Dt. 33:8, Ezra 3:63 & Nm. 27:21).

Our new game came together remarkably fast, and easily, but learning to play it took much longer. At first, I really wasn't sure what to do with it. As it turned out, this game utilized the skills I'd learned in my years with Doris. Using dice, we selected one of our sixteen characters. Then we rolled again to select a relationship to that character. For example, let's say it was the We Bear who is happy, and therefore quite friendly. And let's say the relationship we rolled was "I am happy", indicating an attachment to being happy. It sounds innocent enough, but what we found was not simple, at all. What each game revealed was a long-term emotional block that resulted in avoidance and highly dysfunctional, non-productive behavior. In other words, in this example, holding onto something good would probably be about avoiding something bad, though not necessarily.

While I was describing to each player what their character and relationship meant, I could literally see lights going off within the person playing the game. What made this so powerful was that, while I had no idea what had happened in their life to cause this, I knew exactly what they were doing with it. Once the game triggered a memory in them, I could read their body language, ask a few simple questions, and feel their responses. In this way, I could have more specific information about how their fears were driving them than most psychologists would after dozens of sessions.

I knew from my years with Doris how valuable these personal insights into a person's character structure were, and how hard it normally was to reveal them. All that was good, but there was no way I could teach what Doris had taught me; and without that, there was no game. The way this game accelerated self-awareness was startling to our players, who often felt disoriented by the experience. This was fine, as it was very disarming; but most people simply were not prepared to appreciate the value of piercing their defensive veils this way. The game was lightning fast and deadly accurate, but trust and understanding took longer to develop.

To help you better understand the contents of this game, I will now briefly introduce you to our sixteen characters. Observe in the image below how they match with the chakras and the Lord's Prayer. Feel how they reflect your own experience. Imagine you are seeing reflections of your own personality and observing the secret motives of your subconscious inner child. Can you imagine how seeing what you are going through at this moment is a unique expression of something you've been doing most of your life. Now imagine that the behavior behind this experience is something you are very familiar with, but now you are seeing for the very first time what motivates this behavior. If you can imagine how disturbing this could be if you were not prepared for it, then you may have a pretty good idea of what playing this game was like for us at first.

INTRODUCING THE CHARACTERS

In the Lord's Prayer we see how Spirit fills us from the top (the crown). However, we actually fill with Spirit from the bottom up, like glasses of water. This is why we begin with the Base Chakra. Also, please note that these characters were created to convey the paradigm of good vs. evil, when in truth there are no "good" or "bad" guys. It's all good once we know we are God's Children. To realize our ultimate dream, we must let go of our illusions of good and evil, and that is what this game and the Lord's Prayer are all about.

TERRA & GREEDIE

BASE CHAKRA (Desire)

"And lead us not into temptation but deliver us from evil"

Terra is a princess/gardener who expresses our desire to give, to plant, and to grow. Her nemesis, the Greedie, is a taker who represents our desire to receive. Together, they dance to the law, *"As you plant so shall you reap."* When we attach to Terra or resist the Greedie, their dance stops, and our life force is blocked. As the prayer implies, we are "delivered" from this "evil" as we simply let go. Playing the game just helps to clarify a specific opportunity for letting go that is present right now.

BEAMER & THE GUILTY
NAVEL CHAKRA (Knowing)

"And forgive us our trespasses as we forgive those who trespass against us"

Beamer represents the enthusiasm that comes with trusting in the goodness of our lives. The Guilty represents discernment. Good discernment, or discerning what is good, produces good judgment. Discerning what is bad produces harsh judgment and guilt. Together, trust (Beamer) and discernment (Guilty) enable us to have new experiences and to gain new knowledge and greater freedom. When we become attached or resistant to either discernment or trust, our learning stops. Letting go on this level is accepting the goodness in everything.

WE BEARS & ME BEARS
SOLAR PLEXUS (Responsibility)

"Give us this day our daily bread"

The We Bears are happy, generous, and appreciative. The Me Bears feel isolated, unhappy, and generally disappointed with their daily bread. Both of these bears provide us with valuable insights. However, we are generally attached to feeling happy (We Bears) and resistant to feeling

69

unhappy (the Me Bears). This means that we are also generally ignorant of the valuable information and the powerful emotional forces that these bears offer us to repent, simply changing our point of view to make our lives better. The letting go that allows us to know the wondrous power of these bears is the acceptance of both our positive and negative feelings. They are both blessed resources for making our lives better.

LUVVINS & FEARIES

HEART (Caring)

"Thy kingdom come, thy will be done,
as it is in heaven, so also in earth"

Our fears, The Fearies, are defined by what we care about, as are the Luvvins, who

represent the law of attraction. The Fearies naturally repel, and the Luvvins naturally attract, whatever will honor our deepest caring. Since most of us are following our beliefs and not our hearts, we are unaware of what we truly care most about. This is why we resist our fears (The Fearies) and attach to experiences of attraction (The Luvvins). Not knowing what is really important, we often seem to be repelling what we think we want, and/or attracting what we do not want. This experience undermines our self-esteem and prevents us from realizing the truth, that we are always and everywhere being loved. We reclaim the true compass that these two provide by opening our hearts in gratitude for absolutely everything.

BE-GOOD-BEAGLES
THROAT (Communion)
"Hallowed be thy name"

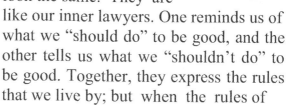

Both Be-Good-Beagles look the same. They are like our inner lawyers. One reminds us of what we "should do" to be good, and the other tells us what we "shouldn't do" to be good. Together, they express the rules that we live by; but when the rules of living become more important than living itself, they no longer serve us. The Bible says that *"For everything there is a season."* To live in the moment, we must be in communion with its spirit. Do you see how when we attach or resist what we believe is right or wrong we are compelled to respond to this moment according to a previous choice? To be fully present, we must be in communion through communicating with this moment. This is how we enjoy our lives. When the rules interfere with this pure enjoyment, it's time to embrace the season at hand and follow our bliss.

LUV-CRYSTAL &
THE BOTTOMLESS-PIT
THIRD EYE (Seeking/Seeing)
"In Heaven"

The Luv-Crystal represents what we value, and the Bottomless Pit is the absence of that. Is the glass half full (Luv-Crystal) or half empty (Bottomless Pit)? Again, these two are intended to guide us toward bliss, but resisting one and/or attaching to the other prevents us from seeing what is. We see what we seek; so, to see God's kingdom *at hand*, we must look without prejudice.

 We can teach our minds to do this by seeking the goodness in everything and everyone. This works, as this is the nature of God's kingdom, which is *at hand*. What doesn't work is trying to define or regulate what the goodness should be. When there is nothing of greater or lesser value, we see the ultimate value of God in everything. The result is peace, and it is in peace that we may truly see.

TRUE-SELF & SLEEZE
CROWN (Identity)
"Our Father"

Sleeze represents our vulnerable, fearful, and defensive self, hiding and or attacking from within his/her armored barrier. He maintains his illusions

 of safety and control like the Wizard of Oz by hiding from anything that might contradict his version of reality. Our True Self is both confident and vulnerable. She/he is free to simply be his or her true self. Together, Sleezes' ability to control or focus, and our True Self's' freedom provides our ability to manifest what we want by focusing on just that. When we attach to or resist either freedom or control, we lose both.

FATHER OF LIGHTS & FEAR-ON
<u>SPIRITUAL HEART</u> (Awareness)
"Our Father"

The Father of Lights represents the Creator aspect of God, and Fear-On is His All-Consuming or destructive nature. Together, these two ultimate forces inspire us to  create and consume by living passionately in the moment. When we resist or attach to either of these primal forces, they are misdirected. Then we forget who we are. We give these God-given powers to other people, places, and things. This is called being obsessed and or addicted. The healing for this ultimate self-betrayal is simply to love everything equally. Love is just the gift of attention, so what you give your attention to will grow. Give your attention to the goodness in everything, claim your freedom to love everything, and it will liberate you to see the kingdom at hand. *Seek first the kingdom of God and all these things shall be added unto you.* That's the promise.

This new game and its delightful characters clearly revealed how we attach to or resist our own life experiences thus revealing opportunities to help us let go and be more present. This is how the Great Spirit honors our deepest caring. We all want to know love, our ever-present Creator. The way into His/Her ever-present kingdom begins with letting go, and our impetus to let go is often called pain. In other words, I'd created a game that not only revealed the nature of each player's most personal suffering, but also showed how they were creating it themselves. Before I tell you about the obvious challenges of sharing this game, I should share the initial success that Barbara, some friends, and myself experienced while playing it.

BARBARA:

When Bodie first began talking about the game, even before there was one, something beautiful and so innocent came over him. For a while, he seemed to be living in another world. He was waking up every night to write down important thoughts and ideas. Sometimes they came in his dreams; at other times he would just wake up thinking and couldn't go back to sleep until he'd written it all down. It was both fascinating and a little frightening to see him so obsessed and so deliberate about something that he could barely describe.

What 'The Game' was, was not clear to me until we played it together. I have to say, playing the game for the first time was a little intimidating. The Game, as we called it, used our fun little characters to reveal deep, very personal experiences. These were not only just too personal to share with other people they were things that we generally don't even want to see within ourselves. How 'The Game' did this so consistently, accurately, and easily was simply amazing! But watching Bodie create it was equally fascinating.

I remember so clearly the first time we played it. When Bodie described what the combination of characters and their positions in my game meant, I was speechless. He kept asking, "Does this mean anything to you?" Each time when I said, "Yes," Bodie looked amazed, because he didn't really know how it was supposed to work, either. I'm guessing that he played this game well over a hundred times with dozens of people before he began to accept what an important and unusual tool he had created.

The Game went right past the details of a person's history and straight to their limiting, irrational feelings and beliefs. It was like shining a bright light into a dark musty old room, so at first it was a little painful and frightening while we adjusted to seeing these darkened inner places. For me, The Game brought back an important series of long-forgotten events that were obviously still affecting me.

As a young girl I was a dancer, and I worked hard at it, but when a real opportunity came along, I was reluctant to be the center of attention. I never knew why, until The Game helped me to understand. Over our next few sessions, it revealed how I was not afraid of the attention, instead, I was concerned about taking it away from anyone else whom I thought needed it more than I. This same thing has happened many times over the course of my life. I've let so many opportunities pass by; and not until I played this game, did I begin to really understand what I was doing, or why.

This may seem like a small thing, but it was, and still is, a very big thing to me. The Game has helped me to identify the irrational source of my fear that permeates my thoughts and affects much of what I create in my life. Seeing this pattern of behavior and the web of thoughts, feelings, and experiences that support it, has been deeply liberating. The loving way that The Game helps me to focus my prayers, while enabling me to acknowledge, heal, and release my self-doubts is astounding.

LEARNING TO PLAY THE GAME

BODIE: By helping me to see the nature of my own feelings of vulnerability and self-doubt, this game was also helping me understand how to share it with others. What the game did was amazing. It quickly penetrated each player's defenses. Then, just as I'd seen in my first vision of it, the game exposed a weak point created by a blockage in his/her unique web of consciousness. While playing the game, some people recalled the trauma that originally created these weak points. For others, remembering didn't seem so important; and they could use the very personal insights to make new choices right away.

Players who were not prepared to appreciate these insights, however, felt exposed, vulnerable, and even violated. The game was exposing their heart-felt pain; and the moment a weak point was identified, most players became completely defensive. Once the walls went up, helping them to see that they could chose to see the weakness differently, and choose to respond differently was very challenging.

HEALING THE PAST

As I was discovering this game, I learned an important lesson beautifully expressed in Hebrews 5:1-3, "*1. For every high priest taken from among men is appointed on behalf of men in things pertaining to God, in order to offer both gifts and sacrifices for sins; 2. he can deal gently with the ignorant and misguided, since he himself also is beset with weakness; 3. and because of it he is obligated to offer sacrifices for sins, as for the people, so also for himself."* (New American Standard Bible). In other words, *Healer, heal thyself.*

One evening while playing this game by myself, it opened a long- forgotten wound. For as long as I could remember, I'd had close relationships with secretive and unhappy people, but I was never aware of what all these people had in common or how much they were really affecting my life. First, the game helped me to recognize how guilty and unworthy I felt in the presence of these people. Then it showed me how I was letting them influence important decisions in ways that were not in my best interest. Such relationships usually began with high hopes but ended with feelings of disappointment, failure, and guilt. My experience of losing the Total Trainer, for example, began and ended with one of these secretive and long-suffering individuals.

During the next few games, I became more and more aware of these nonproductive and unsatisfying relationships. I wondered how and where this all began, so I started tracing my memories farther and farther back. I was amazed at how much of my life was defined by these relationships. How did this all begin? Then one evening, something in the game took me all the way back to the beginning.

I was two-and-a-half years old and at home with my mother. She was obviously deeply depressed, and I was feeling guilty. I was compelled to know what I'd done to cause her such pain. If I only knew, I was certain I could make her feel better. I pleaded with her, "What's wrong, Mommy? What did I do?" Then she turned towards me. Her face was bright red and she screamed, "Go to your room and just wait until you're an adult, then you'll find out how hard it is." No wonder I was so eager to take Peter Pan's oath!

I was still projecting my toddler's completely unfounded fears and guilt into my current relationships. I wasn't just attracting secretive or hurt people, I was actually looking for these traits in everyone. How crazy is that? Perhaps if there'd been a wise, loving, and reassuring adult present when I was two, my life's journey would have been very different. It's impossible to say. But playing this game has helped to make me a wiser, more loving, and reassuring adult companion to this child who is still within me.

WHAT IS "SPIRITUAL?"

Most of the people who came to play our "spiritual healing game" didn't have much actual experience with either spirituality or healing. After a really good game, we would rejoice at hearing things like, *"I just learned more in an hour than I did in five years of therapy."* In truth, however, the people who were already very devoted to self-improvement received the greatest benefits. With these people, I often felt like the last guy who easily opens the jar after a dozen others have tried. It was very obvious that a lot had gone into loosening that lid before I got my turn.

Most players were shocked by how quickly the game stripped away their defenses. It revealed core beliefs that had been eroding their self-esteem for most of their lives. When they gave us the chance, we could often help them to see how these beliefs were needlessly separating them from what they really wanted. Then, if they were still up for it, we would show them how applying the Lord's Prayer to these memories could transform what seemed like a curse, into a blessing? But this seldom happened.

Ironically, the better I got at playing The Game, the more I heard our players say, "*This isn't a game,*" or "*This isn't fun.*" Well, the game of life isn't fun when we take ourselves too seriously but try sharing that with someone who is suffering. Try helping someone who feels like a victim accept creative responsibility for what they are experiencing. Before you try, you might want to put on some protective padding!

Fortunately, we have now refined and produced a way to play 'The Game' in the privacy of your own home gaining insight from the wisdom of your souls loving inner awareness. If you would like to try it Join Us at seeyourselfloving.com

PART IV
"THE ANCIENT ONES"

"YOU ARE THE LIGHT OF THE WORLD"

As this chapter begins, our journey takes some surprising new turns towards exotic ideas and people. They lead us into magical worlds, which are built on the idea that we are the lights of the world. Can you imagine a whole culture working in one accord to express *"let there be light?"* Would it ever occur to you, or could you imagine, that there is a connection between the ancient

Mayans and Jesus? Can you conceive of previous civilizations on earth whose technological abilities were superior to our own today? These are just some of the mind-bending questions that we confront as we travel through this next part of our story.

It is one thing to entertain such thoughts from a safe distance but seeing is believing. Believing is "being and living," and herein you will see actual proof that there is more happening on our planet and within ourselves than most of us are courageous or creative enough to imagine. What makes this part of our book so important is that, to expand the boundaries of our human experiences, we must also expand the boundaries of our imaginations. Though we made these discoveries many years ago, they continue to change our views and our experiences of each day because we have learned to translate these discoveries into actual experiences. We will share these with you in Part VII.

If you open your mind to believe it is possible, then you too will have a new experience of life. This is the whole point of our book. Our purpose is to offer exercises to experientially reveal the promise of the Lord's Prayer within you. Your experiences will expand the boundaries of your imagination, but imagination will also give you permission to have these experiences. They go hand in hand. As you will see, the fruit of our own imagination, The Game, opened the way for us to enter this most extraordinary new/ancient world.

THE GAME BOARD
One night, after playing a particularly challenging game with some especially defensive friends, my inner voice suggested, "Maybe a game board would help." That

sounded great to me. Creating a game board would be enjoyable, and it was a good excuse to take a break from playing and thinking about The Game so much. I quickly made several designs using our sixteen characters, and they were beautiful but not magical. The magic began one particularly boring evening at my Sunday job as a barker in the amusement games on the Santa Monica Pier.

The weather was cold and drizzly, so we had very few customers. To pass the time, I was spinning quarters on my counter. I was watching a quarter spin, when I got an idea for a new game board. When I got home that evening, I took a large mixing bowl from our kitchen and a bag full of quarters to our bedroom. About an hour later, there was a magnificent pattern of 474 quarters laid

out on our bedroom floor. Arranged that way, the quarters seemed to shimmer and dance as if they were alive (see fig.). I called Barbara, who was equally impressed, and we both stood there entranced by the breathing rhythms of this extraordinary design. Over the next few weeks, we saw many symbols, patterns, and numbers that were meaningful to us within our new game board. The seven larger, unbroken continuous circles in the pattern contained 294 spheres. Numerology teaches that this is the number for Melchizedek, the most mysterious figure in the Bible, is 294. The total spheres in the pattern numbers 474; and 474 is the number that represents Daath. Daath is the invisible seraph on the Tree of Life is one of the greatest mysteries of the Hebrew Kabala. So instead of adding clarity to our game, this new game board brought even more mystery to it. I spent weeks analyzing, researching, and thinking about how these symbols and what they seem to imply could be used to improve The Game. The result, however, was that the game became so complex, that even I was confused.

Still, I was completely fascinated by the promise of this new game board, so I couldn't just let it go, as I had

with our previous game boards. Instead, I decided to follow my first instinct and just meditate with it for a while. It made a wonderful Yantra, which is a sacred visual design to evoke states of inner spiritual awareness. Using it this way, I quickly discovered that my instincts were right. It was indeed a wonderful tool for open-eye meditations; and during one of my meditations with it, a spider appeared.

Spider reminded me of my original vision of The Game, teaching us to use our webs of consciousness the way a spider does. Spider waits, meditating until her web attracts what she needs, and this is exactly what meditation is all about. What the spider does is like seeking first the kingdom of God (within) so all her needs may be added unto her. Then I saw the six-points at the center of the game board as the Hebrew symbol, the Star of David. I didn't understand why I was seeing all these images in our game board, but I felt that they were leading me somewhere, and I was willing to just follow.

THE STAR IN THE PRAYER

About a week after seeing the star within the spider in our game board, I saw the very same thing in the Lord's Prayer. I was studying the two places in the New Testament where Jesus taught the Lord's Prayer. As we stated in the preface, it first appears in Matthew 6:9-13 and then in Luke 11:1-4. Jesus was not just offering an example of how to pray, but also actually teaching this specific prayer. I learned that most experts agree that the  prayer in Luke is the original, and that they believe the longer ending in Matthew was added later. This made sense, as Luke's version aligns perfectly with the seven chakras and seven original branches of Yoga, while the version in Matthew does not.

It was within the subtle differences in the heart of the prayer that I saw this star. Matthew reads, "Thy kingdom come, Thy will be done, on earth as it is in heaven." Luke reads, "Thy kingdom come, Thy will be done, as it is in heaven so also in earth." Do you see the difference? Does it seem important? Most people, myself included, would say it doesn't. Luke's version, however,

1. Thy Kingdom
6. So also in Earth
2. Come
5. As it is in Heaven
3. Thy Will
4. Be Done

in perfect geometric proportion, produces a six-pointed breathing star. Again, this made sense as the prayer is about us, and we are the light of the world. When I saw this, I naturally thought of the star in the spider and wondered what it all meant. Though I didn't see the meaning, it did seem important, and again I felt that I was being guided somewhere.

HARMONIC CONVERGENCE

The game board seemed to have opened the way for a whole new type of discovery. Where it was leading or what it would reveal wasn't clear yet, but at the same time I was rekindling another of my childhood fascinations. Looking through my grandmother's National Geographic magazines as a child, I absolutely knew I would visit the Mayan temples in Mexico one day. In those pictures I saw a world rich with imagination that inspired wonder, and I imagined what it would be like to have lived in such a marvelous world of pageantry. I didn't like to read and was criticized by my parents and teachers as being too imaginative, so I kept my fantasies to myself. Fortunately, I had no idea about the bloody sacrificial ceremonies that the later Mayans had performed.

In 1987, when I read José Arguelles' book The Mayan Factor, my childhood fascination was quickly revived. One of the first things I read was that there were two distinctly different Mayan civilizations. José believed that the early civilization had not participated in blood sacrifices. In fact, according to their ancient stories, Mayas had a civilization more advanced than our own. These stories say that the first Mayans were galactic Travelers from the Pleiades, who come to earth to help us prepare for the dawning of a new era. The ending of the Tzolkin, their 26,000-year calendar, marks the beginning of this new era, on December 21, 2012 A.D. The Mayan calendar, José believed, could help prepare us for our imminent transition into this new era.

The Mayan Factor described the Maya's advanced esoteric, mathematical, and astronomical knowledge. Together with their evolved benevolent intent, this knowledge enabled them to calculate and predict a sequence of auspicious events leading to a climactic conclusion. He further believed that holding pure intentions collectively during these auspicious times would accelerate our own personal and collective evolution into this fast-approaching new reality. The first of these auspicious moments was August 17, 1987, which José called the "Harmonic Convergence." José's vision captured us, and on that day Barbara and I joined millions of others who were holding thoughts of peace and prosperity for the new era. This experience stirred a new kind of hope within me, and though I wasn't looking for it, I also saw a remote, yet definite connection between the ancient Mayas and the Lord's Prayer.

Both the Mayan and Hindu calendars, the Tzolkin and the Kali-Yuga, are 26,000 years long. Both calendars end at about the same time, coinciding with the apocalyptic timeline in the Bible, and, like the Bible, both end with the beginning of a heavenly new reality and both align with the dawning of the "Age of Aquarius." The first records of Yoga are found in Hindu scriptures written over 5,000 years ago. As you know, the seven roots of Yoga have contributed generously to our understanding of the Lord's Prayer. It wasn't enough to draw conclusions, but it did make me wonder.

A PROPHECY

On February 17, 1989, my 40th birthday, Barbara gave me $1,700 to attend an Insight Training seminar. But if you want to make God laugh, tell Her your plans. The next day, our new friends Saivahni and Atona announced that they were going on a "spiritual journey" tour to the Mayan Temples in Mexico. I hadn't thought much about the Mayas since the Harmonic Convergence; but the moment I heard about this trip to Mexico, I was all ears. They said the tour was being led by Hunbatz-Men, a Mayan Elder, whom I remembered from José Arguelles' book. Hunbatz-Men had helped José understand the significance of the Harmonic Convergence. Now Hunbatz was taking over a hundred people, including José Arguelles and Jose's wife, Lloydine, on this trip. He was to perform the first traditional ceremonies in the Mayan temples since the invading Spaniards had forbidden them five hundred years earlier. We were fascinated!

When Saivahni said the trip cost $1,700, I knew that Barbara and I were going, too. This was a completion of the prophecy I'd felt as a child looking at Gramma's magazines. Since embracing the Lord's Prayer, our lives had steadily grown richer, fuller, more rewarding, and happier, but raising seven kids in L.A. is a big job. In twelve years, we'd vacationed only once together, and only for two days. Leaving for two weeks seemed impossible, but all the pieces of this hugely optimistic adventure came together quickly, joyfully, and effortlessly.

Soon we were meeting with our fellow travelers, many of whom had been studying and preparing for this trip since the Harmonic Convergence. The first thing we learned was that performing ceremonies in the Mayan temples was still against the law in Mexico! For the next month, Barbara and I attended at least three classes a week, some taught by Hunbatz-Men himself. We learned about the Ancient Ones, the mysterious founders of the Mayan culture; and the more we learned, the more excited we became. We fasted and practiced celibacy in preparation for our upcoming adventure, and suddenly we were there.

Our journey through the Yucatan with Hunbatz-Men began in Palenque, a village founded by K'uk' B'ahlam on March 11, 431 A.D. As we walked among Palenque's exquisite stone temples, it was easy to imagine, and even feel, the magical world of these Ancient Ones. The surrounding jungle, teeming with the sounds of exotic birds, jaguars, monkeys, and insects, perfectly accentuated our otherworldly experience. We were mesmerized, and the sacred presence that we felt there inspired us to pray and meditate often. Every day we were there, opened us to something new, inspiring and deeply uplifting. Best of all, in just four short days, Barbara and I were bonded, as people are, when they have shared something so personal, powerful, sacred, and life-changing.

TEMPLE OF THE SUN

On our last day in Palenque, Barbara and I awoke before dawn, and I had the strong sense that I was missing something important. I felt as if I had come a long way to get something, but I knew I hadn't gotten it yet, and time was running out. I didn't even know what "it" was, until our final sunrise ceremony at Temple of the Sun. As the sun was peeking over the awakening jungle canopy, we found ourselves standing in front of the Sun Cross Codex. I began feeling extremely unworthy, and I started to pray.

As I said the Lord's Prayer, a faint tingling sensation began in my hands and feet. It continued and  grew, until my whole body was vibrating. Then I saw a golden burst of light, and the vibrating stopped. I felt weightless, and then I was falling and being lifted at the same time. My years of experience with Mantra Yoga had taught me to let go when my instincts were just the opposite. The more I let go, the deeper I fell, and the higher I seemed to rise. Finally, I came to a vision of golden waves of light pulsing from a sun that was rising over a pyramid. Unbeknownst to me, Barbara was having a vision of her own at the same time.

THE GODDESS

BARBARA: As Bodie and I slowly walked up the steps of Temple of the Sun that morning I felt the same reverence I'd felt as a child walking toward the altar of our church for Holy Communion. Here, though, it was as though I were stepping into another reality. A sacred place that felt inviting, lovingly comforting, and yet strange and unfamiliar. As I approached the massive codex carved on a great slab of stone, my eyes defocused. I was trying to see the inscriptions, but quickly everything started to fade into a golden light.

My knees got weak. I remember saying the Lord's Prayer, then chanting, as I felt someone gently guiding me  to a place to sit down. My eyes were so heavy I couldn't open them, and yet the light was blindingly bright. When the light began to dim, I began seeing into a different world; different, but still the same. With my eyes closed, I could see the jungle across the hillside and people interacting just down from where I was sitting. I heard birds singing, but it was like hearing and seeing them through a television screen with waves of energy flowing across it.

The frame of the screen grew and grew, and I realized that I was the one tuning in the picture. Not only was I tuning it in, I was using the gentle motions of my eight arms to move the energy and create the picture I wanted to see. Whoa! Eight arms! Where did they come from? I shifted the picture to reveal our children, whom I could see and hear perfectly, and I felt my heart open even bigger. The intense love I was feeling was literally overwhelming, and I lost consciousness. A block of time went by before I again noticed my many arms. Then, as though looking back at myself, I saw the most beautiful goddess I have ever imagined or have ever seen in pictures.

She was wearing a headdress adorned with magnificent jewels and a softly flowing garment that moved ever so gently with the slightest breeze. Her arms were in constant movement, as though she were dancing with God, delicately creating newness with each movement. I was spellbound by what I saw and deliciously savoring the experience of being in two places at once. At some point, I realized that I was the dancing goddess, and the observer, witnessing the beauty of creation unfolding before me. Never before, nor since have I had such a realistic, tactile experience in meditation, and it's as real for me now as it was then.

Nearly an hour went by before I began to come back from the dance, still seated on the stairs of Temple of the Sun. What had just happened? Was I in a trance? Had this beautiful goddess really been me in some other life? Or was she still a part of me now? What just happened, and what does it all mean? I had no idea. But I did know that my perception of reality had changed. I knew that other realities do co-exist, and that I had literally stood between two worlds! Amazed as I was at what had just happened, I knew it was equally important to let it go and continue being open to whatever came next.

THE SUN CROSS CODEX

As we emerged from these experiences, Barb and I heard our fellow travelers playing indigenous instruments from all over the world. We danced in the temple and down the temple steps. We strolled together through the beautiful grounds of Palenque until we came to a young

Mayan artist from Guatemala. He was selling handmade replicas of the Sun Cross Codex, and we listened as he described its meaning.

(SUN CROSS CODEX)

The young man said that the figure on the left was Lord' Pacal, who ascended the throne at age 12 on the 29th of July 615, and lived to the age of 80. Pacal reigned as king and high priest of Palenque for 67 years. He initiated a building program that produced some of the Mayan civilization's finest art and architecture. After his death, Pacal the Great was worshiped as a god, and he was said to have communicated with his descendants. Across from him in the codex was Pacal's son, Chan Bahlam, who succeeded him as king. The square image in the center of the codex was Hunab Ku, God of the Central Sun. Pacal and his son were making their offering to Hunaba Ku in preparation for Chan Bahlam's initiation into the royal Mayan priesthood.

As the young artist spoke, my attention was drawn to their offerings or sacrifices; and I wondered if these represented our fight or flight animal instincts. What if the messages of both Jesus and the Mayas were the same? What if they both taught that the hardness of our hearts is the obstacle to our spiritual growth that must be sacrificed before we may ascend or live as spiritual beings? This is what playing the game also appeared to reveal. It seemed that very few were even aware of this hardness or defensiveness, so it was not surprising that the later Mayas

would have misinterpreted this teaching. It wasn't hard to see how they may have misunderstood that, to appease the gods, they must actually cut out and offer human hearts.

As I looked at the offerings in the codex, I saw that they were being held as if they had come out of their hearts. I saw, within the story that the young artist was telling, a deeper spiritual teaching very similar to those embedded in the Lord's Prayer. When I asked him about this, however, he became quiet and insisted that this was all he knew. As a memento of our experiences at Temple of the Sun that morning, Barb and I bought one of his replicas of the Sun Cross Codex. Over the years, it has helped to keep our memories of these experiences alive.

MELCHIZEDEK

In a class just before the trip, Hunbatz-Men said that the Ancient Ones had come to earth at eight different times and places. In each time and place, they were known by different names. As we were preparing to leave Palenque, I was already seeing this as a possible explanation of how and why the seven roots of Yoga could be so present in the Lord's Prayer, and why Jesus and the Mayan Ancient Ones may have taught something very similar. I was reminded of Melchizedek, whose number, 294, was among the first messages we had received from our game board. It seemed rather perfect that he would be part our journey to discover the magical promise of the Lord's Prayer.

When Melchizedek's number appeared in our game board, we tried to learn everything we could about him, hoping that he could shed some new light on our game. Like the Mayan myths about the Ancient Ones, the Bible tells us enough about Melchizedek to be certain that he existed and was very important, but even the authors of the Bible were mystified by him. For example, the chapter where he appears in Hebrews is a mystery. Except for John 1, it is the only chapter of the New Testament whose author is unknown. It says that Melchizedek was the King of Salem, which is thought to be Jerusalem, and that Jesus was ordained forever a priest after the order of Melchizedek (Hebrews 5: 6). What does that mean? Such an order is defined as "a group of persons living under a religious rule." This seems to imply that Melchizedek was a king and priest whose spiritual authority was honored, respected, and adhered to by Jesus. How is it possible that neither Barbara nor I had ever heard his name mentioned in our churches?

In Genesis 14:18, Melchizedek is called the Priest of El Elyon, the Most High God, which would be like Our Father who art in heaven. Then he is described as blessing Abraham in the name of El Elyon, and Abraham gives Melchizedek a tithe. This act of tithing means that Abraham also recognized Melchizedek as his own spiritual authority. Evidently, the spiritual empowerment of Abraham, the father of the Hebrew nation, and that of Jesus are both attributed to Melchizedek. How does someone so important remain so anonymous? Is this a conspiracy, or is it a testimony to how adamantly most of us avoid what we cannot understand?

In our attempts to understand who Melchizedek really was, we came across other mysteries which also raised questions for us. For example, the word Elohim is used in the bible 2,222 times. It is translated as "God" or "The Lord God," but it also refers to a plurality of gods. When Adam and Eve were expelled from the Garden of Eden, for example, The Lord God (Elohim) said, "behold the man has become as one of us knowing good and evil." Who is "us"? It certainly sounds as if there were some gods in the garden. Who were they, and what does this mean?

To us, this all meant that our churches seemed to be intentionally and selectively omitting anything that they could not explain. When I was seven, I was even labeled a heretic by Monsignor Ott in an effort to frighten my mother and silence me. It worked until I was an adult, when the obvious closed-mindedness of churches encouraged me to look for what they may have missed or avoided. The more we searched, the more we found. Barb and I could only conclude that, if they were avoiding Melchizedek, they might also be avoiding the Ancient Ones, also described as gods, for the same reasons.

THE ANCIENT ONES

After our experiences at Temple of the Sun, Barbara and I both felt as if something we did there had connected us with what had been done there long ago by the Ancient Ones. Naturally, we wanted to know what that was, and our fellow travelers in Mexico were knowledgeable and very helpful. However, no one seemed to have any insight into the meaning of the original ceremonies performed at Temple of the Sun. Luckily, as we were leaving Palenque on our tour bus, Barbara and I sat next to a fascinating and very intelligent young lady named Arleen. As we wound our way through the mountains of Chiapas on our way to the sacred caverns of Loltun, Arleen, Barbara, and I had a fascinating and very enlightening conversation.

In answer to our questions about Temple of the Sun, Arleen offered us a particularly valuable insight. She said she believed that the Maya's vast knowledge of the cosmos and its significance to our lives was like the gift-wrapping on their real prize. "The cosmos," she said, "is just a reflection of our inner selves. I believe they understood how to use their knowledge of the stars to guide and elevate their inner awareness, and this is how they were able to realize their godlike potential."

I was completely amazed, as she seemed to be describing the Lord's Prayer. It seemed to be about Our Father in the heavens above, but in truth was designed to reveal how we humans are created in the image and likeness of God. Before I could catch my breath, Arleen moved on and began talking about the Anasazi, who were the forbearers of the Navaho, Zuni, Hopi, and Ute Native American tribes. "The Hopi tell stories of a 'Red City' far to the south," she said, "where their youth were trained to become the shamans and chiefs of their tribes. We know now that the walls and temples of Palenque were once painted a bright red."

Arlene continued, "In Navajo, Anasazi actually means 'Ancient Ones', and the Anasazi and Mayan myths are very similar. Both say that their Ancient Ones were highly evolved souls from the Pleiades, who came to earth by entering the wombs of human mothers. This merged their destinies with ours, allowing them to express their evolved arts, philosophies, and sciences of their home worlds. Both the Mayan and Anasazi myths even agree that, when their mission on earth was completed, the Ancient Ones ascended to the Seven Heavens from which they came."

Arleen's passion for truth was revealing the connectedness of the Mayan and Anasazi civilizations. "Their myths are thought of as fantasies," she said, "though they explain what we cannot." As Arleen expressed her passion for the secrets of the Ancient Ones, it seemed that we were drawn together by the magnetism of our purposes. On the bus ride, Barbara and I played "The Game" with her, for which she was deeply grateful, as it helped her to make an important life decision that she'd been struggling with.

I told Arleen how this idea of the Ancient Ones being gods from other worlds reminded me of Melchizedek. I wasn't really surprised to hear that she had studied him, as well. I was, however, deeply impressed to hear her recite Hebrews 7: 3: *He is the king of peace; Without father, without mother, without descent, having neither beginning of days, nor end of life; but made like unto the Son of God; abideth a priest continually. Now consider how great this man was unto whom even the patriarch Abraham gave a tenth of the spoils.*

THE WHEEL

I knew that our own archeologists and historians could not explain how or why either the Mayan or Anasazi cultures had vanished. Nor did they know how the Mayas, a primitive, stone-age culture that did not even use the wheel, could have produced such advanced art, architecture, mathematics, astronomy, and social/political systems. I was a little puzzled by the wheel thing myself. Again, Arleen had a beautifully revealing answer to this important question.

"We know that the ancient Mayas were exceptional astronomers, whose fascination with time enabled them to create the most complex and accurate calendar in history," she said. "We know that they understood time as an intricate system of interlocking circular realities, wherein God, humans, and nature are meshed in perpetual concert.

Obviously, they knew what a wheel was and were capable of imagining how it might be useful.

"I believe the reason they didn't use it was to send this critical message: the wheel is sacred. Its use for accomplishing menial tasks has led to our current industrialization and technology and the catastrophic results that we are just now seeing."

After our long conversation, I realized that our friends Arlene and Atona were the two who had first recognized that Barbara and I were experiencing something inexplicably powerful at Temple of the Sun that morning. The many conversations that we had with both Arleen, and with Atona afterwards, helped us begin integrating what we had experienced there.

PART V
"JESUS IS FAST"
$(J = mc^2)$

WONDERLAND

Barbara and I experienced Mexico like Alice experienced Wonderland. We'd learned just enough to stimulate our imaginations, and what we imagined closely resembled what we experienced. We expected to enter the remnants of a once-magical world designed and dedicated to announcing, teaching, and celebrating the spiritual evolution of humanity. Actually, being there expanded our imaginations, until we fully believed in the accuracy of their ancient myths. The fact that our fellow travelers were much more knowledgeable about the Maya than we were made us feel even more like children. To us, their world was still a truly magical kingdom and remarkably alive. It was like an old apple tree bearing its most delicious fruit, though its trunk and branches are worn and decayed with age.

We went there in search of Mayan treasure, and we found it quite by accident at Temple of the Sun. Eventually, in the Sun Cross Codex, we would see a spiritual map similar to the Lord's Prayer. Comparing these two maps of human consciousness would illuminate more than we imagined then; but to see it this way, we had to go deeper. Our experiences in Mexico were like appetizers. As we flew back to Los Angeles, it was obvious that Mexico was the beginning of a new chapter in our lives.

DURANGO

After spending nearly two weeks in Mexico immersed in fruitful conversations, heart-felt prayers, and high meditations, we were thoroughly enchanted. Even before returning home, we'd decided to seriously entertain the possibility of moving our family to Durango, Colorado, where the Anasazi civilization once thrived. A few weeks after returning home, Barbara and I visited Durango. Just the idea of moving there made us feel light and free, and on our second day there, we placed a bid on a new home. A month later, our home in Venice Beach was sold, and we prepared to move with our two dogs, two cats, one hamster, seven children, and number eight, Azza, on the way.

BARBARA: We both saw this moment in time (our experiences with the prayer thus far, Mexico, the Ancient Ones, the prophecies, and Azza's impending arrival) as a window of opportunity that would not remain open long. Bodie grew up in San Diego, and we'd both lived in Los Angeles for nearly twenty years. I, however, grew up in Sonora, a small town in Northern California. I loved my childhood, the beauty of the surrounding mountains, and the small-town caring for others that I had experienced there. This was how I'd dreamt of raising our children. Not only did this move make sense to me, it was an answer to my prayers. When Bodie and I went to Durango to visit and look for a new home, I had two most unusual experiences that convinced me even more that this move was right.

On our first day there, Bodie and I hiked in a gorgeous aspen grove in the mountains just outside of town. We sat down to pray and give thanks for all the blessings that we were being showered with. First, I prayed, and then I listened. As the subtle winds blew through the aspens, I heard a voice. It startled me and I opened my eyes, but no one was there. Then I realized that it came from inside me. It clearly said, "Hello, my name is Azza, I am the angel within you." I assumed this Azza was my guardian angel, until we were back in Los Angeles. When I realized I was pregnant again, the "angel within me" took on a whole other meaning! Who was this child who introduced himself and even showed me how to spell his name? And why had he chosen that time and place to introduce himself?

SACRED GEOMETRY

The second thing that convinced me Durango would be our new home were the experiences we had in

the Anasazi kivas at Mesa Verde I felt a wonderful sense of sacredness there. While praying and meditating in the Sun Temple kiva at Mesa Verde (see picture), we were both reminded of our experiences at Temple of the Sun in Palenque. That's when we both knew that we'd made the right decision. We couldn't explain this to our friends or family; we didn't even try. But our instincts were right. Our experiences there over the next three years were some of the most magical and blessed times of our lives.

When we returned from Durango, as we were packing to move, our friend Arleen, whom we'd met in Mexico, showed up unexpectedly at our door. She was very excited to share with us a Flower of Life workshop she'd just taken. In Mexico, we showed her our new game board, and I remember how she stared at it the same way Bodie and I did the first time we saw it. That's why Arleen came to see us. The workshop she'd just taken was about something called "sacred geometry", and she said the Flower of Life reminded her of our game board. Then

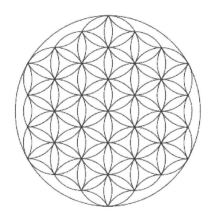

she told us that sacred geometry was the basis of all religions and high cultures, and that it was used in building the Egyptian and Mayan temples. What she said reminded us of the sacred science which Ralph De Bitt had spoken of in his book.

FLOWER OF LIFE

BODIE: Arleen's surprise visit came at just the right moment, and she said several things that day that interested us. First was the idea that a sacred science was the basis of all religions. Then she said that the teacher of this class believed that this spiritual science had originated with the Order of Melchizedek. Finally, Arleen told us that the Flower of Life workshop concluded with a very unique meditation, which incorporated breathing and sacred geometry to activate our human energy fields. The way she described it felt very similar to how I was experiencing and seeing the Lord's Prayer. I was signed up for the next Flower of Life workshop before Arleen left our house that day.

The boxes were still unpacked and our new home in a state of chaos, with our older children robustly rebelling about moving to a "hick town that didn't even have a real shopping mall." Nevertheless, with Barbara's encouragement and blessing, I left Durango to take my first course in sacred geometry, while she handled the uprising and the unpacking.

Over the next few days, my brain slowly turned to mush as our sacred geometry teacher, Drunvalo, introduced us to the six-thousand-year-old Flower of Life design. He showed us how the world's greatest thinkers, philosophers, artists, and architects had utilized it in their masterpieces. Cathedrals, temples, and pyramids were built with the sacred science it contains. Even the original Hebrew temple, the Holy of Holies, and the Arc of the Covenant were built with it. So were Solomon's Temple, the Great Pyramid, and the Mayan and ancient Grecian temples. The philosophy of Plato, the mathematical genius of Pythagoras, the art and innovations of Leonardo De Vinci, and the music of Beethoven were all created with this sacred science.

By connecting the key points and lines within the Flower of life, important symbols were clearly revealed: the Hebrew Tree of Life, the Sanskrit Om and Hu symbols, the Oriental yin/yang symbol, and the Islamic cube (see images). These symbols alone represent over 75% of our world's faiths, and there were many more.

SYMBOLS IN THE FLOWER OF LIFE

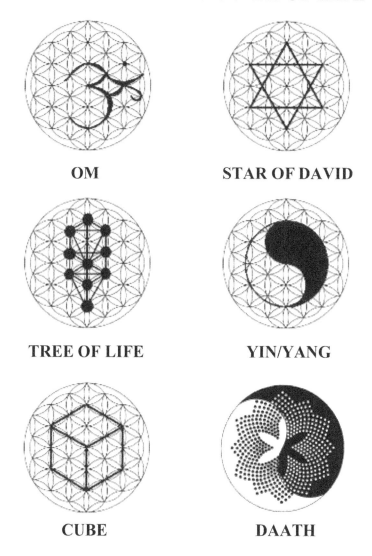

OM

STAR OF DAVID

TREE OF LIFE

YIN/YANG

CUBE

DAATH

Drunvalo described the Flower of Life as the "fabric of creation," and all that it contained seemed to

point to one magnificent form. It was a three-dimensional, eight-pointed star, called the "Star-Tetrahedron." This star (see fig. left) is present within the formations of all new life forms, including the human embryo, and the crystalline structures of rocks and minerals. Drunvalo also showed us how this star is present within the structures of our sun and its planets. It is also clearly implied in Leonardo de Vinci's Vitruvian Man (see fig. right).

THE HOLY TRINITY

After that workshop, on my way back to Durango, while driving over the Continental Divide, I envisioned how connecting the three sections of the Lord's Prayer also described a star-tetrahedron.

- The three chakras above the heart form a heavenly triad defining who God is *(Our Father)*, where He is *(in heaven)*, and how to worship Him (*Hallowed be thy name*).
- The three lower chakras form a second triad about our earthly needs for *daily bread, forgiveness, and deliverance.*

- Finally, as we've already shown, the third section in the heart chakra defines a six-pointed star.

This star is made of two overlapping triads symbolizing the unity of heaven and earth as in *"thy kingdom come, thy will be done, as it is in heaven so also in earth"*. Merging the heavenly and earthly triads into

this star in the heart produces a star-tetrahedron. The creation of this eight-pointed star defines the Holy Trinity: Father (above), Son (below), and the Holy Spirit (The Light) of God's Will that unites these within our human hearts.

GOD'S SIGNATURE

Today, we call this star-tetrahedron within the Lord's Prayer, God's signature. We call it this because it literally translates the intent of this prayer into a symbol, which our inner child already knows and understands. Not only does this star describe the unity of

heaven and earth, it also presents a simple, childlike understanding of how this seemingly impossible goal is accomplished. We believe that placing this star in the prayer served in the same way that name or brand recognition does in advertising. By using God's signature in this way, our inner child is immediately sold on the goodness and integrity of the Lord's Prayer. We believe this star is an example of what Jesus meant when he said in *LUKE 18:16-17, "16 But Jesus called them unto him, and said, Suffer little children to come unto me, and forbid them not: for of such is the nature of the kingdom of God. 17: Verily I say unto you, whosoever shall not receive the kingdom of God as a little child shall in no wise enter therein."* In other words, leading our inner child to the Christ within us is perhaps a purpose of the Lord's Prayer.

Feelings and imagery are languages that the child understands, and the eight-pointed star contains even more graphic insights and information for guiding our inner child to Christ. By simply reconnecting the eight points of a star-tetrahedron differently, a cube is created (see image.). The star (a symbol of light) embedded in a cube (a symbol of the material world) affirms what science has just discovered, and spiritual masters 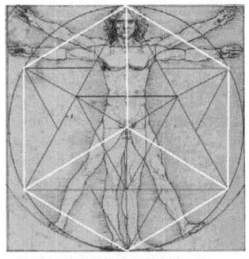 have been saying all along: The material world is made of light. So, to *be the light of the world*, to realize God's kingdom is *at hand*, we just reconnect our dots differently. The Lord's Prayer and our game are both about how we realize that *"we are the light of the world"* and that *"the kingdom of God is at hand."*

JESUS IS FAST

One day I was sitting in my office contemplating the implications of the two stars within the prayer, when our then four-year-old son, Shawn, came bursting through the door. His eyes were ablaze with excitement, and he was breathing heavily. He took a deep breath and said, "Dad, I want to be just like Jesus!" I have never preached to our kids. I have wanted them to discover God in their own ways, as I have. I assumed Shawn had been talking to the preacher next door, and I asked him why he wanted to be "just like Jesus." Shawn's eyes got even bigger, as if to say, "Don't you know?" Still out of breath, he gasped, *"Dad, Jesus is fast!"*

I was both amazed and stunned. At the very moment when Shawn burst in, I was thinking of Albert Einstein's theory of relativity ($E=mc^2$), which states that time and space are not absolutes, but are relative to the speed of light. I was wondering if Albert Einstein had created an actual equation mathematically explaining how and why *God's kingdom will come when His will* (let there be light) *is done.* These were my exact thoughts as Shawn burst into my office that afternoon to inform me, *"Jesus is fast."*

Before my head had stopped spinning, Shawn was out the door, back on his bike, and riding down the hill as fast as his little legs would allow. I took his dramatic entry at that very moment and his proclamation as an affirmation that God's will can indeed be mathematically calculated. Then I understood that this was also the purpose behind the Maya's developing their ultra-sophisticated mathematical system. The presence of these stars and the chakras in the Lord's Prayer affirm that our physical, mental, and emotional bodies are created as mechanisms for helping us realize and utilize the potential of the light within us. Albert Einstein predicted mathematically what Jesus and the Ancient Ones demonstrated. This is also what Jesus was talking about when he said, *'You are the light of the world,"* *"You are gods,"* and *"You shall do even greater things than these."*

ATONEMENT

As a young child in the Catholic Church, I was taught that the purpose of the Lord's Prayer was for atonement, which I understood to be our punishment for being both bad and human. The Church taught that we are born with original sin, so we are naturally sinful. I was taught that I must confess my sins to be forgiven. After confession, the priest would ask if I was sorry, and I would say, "Yes." Then he would say, "Now for your penance, say ten Our Fathers & ten Hail Mary's and go in peace." As I got bigger, so did my sins, for which I had to atone with a larger number of prayers.

Naturally, I grew up associating prayer with punishment. That's why I am so amazed at how closely what I was taught then actually resembles what I believe now. Today, I understand that it is our outwardly focused five senses that cause us to miss the mark, or sin. How we fail to get what we truly want, which is unconditional love, as we are seduced by our five senses is like original sin. The importance of acknowledging our failures is like confessing our sins. And, when we break down the word "atonement" we see "at-one-ment." So, what we see, and experience truly is defined by how we connect the dots.

I am amazed at how close this new understanding, which lifts me up and sets me free, is so close to the demeaning misinterpretation of the church that once made me feel so guilty and worthless. What this tells me is how important our intentions are. As we pray, connecting the loving thoughts that the Lord's Prayer defines, I believe it is crucial that we stay focused on the light, which each part of this prayer expresses in a unique way. As we take our journey along the "middle path," and as we enter the "narrow gate," this light becomes more subtle and pure. What is so subtle and pure is easily corrupted, so we must be watchful that we are not doing the right thing for the wrong reason. In fact, our realities are not defined as much by what we do as why we do it.

WHAT IF THE UNIVERSE IS A HOLOGRAM?

Soon after taking that first sacred geometry course, Barb and I were given a fascinating book, *The Holographic Universe*. In it the author, Michael Talbot, weaves the revolutionary thesis of cutting-edge scientists, psychologists, and theologians that our universe is really the ultimate hologram. Mr. Talbot helps us to see how holograms defy the linear cause and effect law of science, which says; *"for every action there is an equal and opposite reaction,"* just as Albert Einstein predicted. As the "cause and effect" thesis defies the basis of our Western sciences, religions, and legal systems, most authorities naturally reject this holographic theory, as it explains what they cannot.

Mr. Talbot described how splitting a laser, a pure light, is the first step toward creating a hologram, which is very similar to how the Bible describes the beginning of creation. In Genesis 1, it says, *God says let there be light,* and then, *God created the heaven and the earth, God divided the light from the darkness, God created firmament to divided the waters from the waters, and* He *divided the day from the night.* Is Moses, the author of Genesis, describing how God created the universe like a hologram? If we can create holograms with a man-made light, certainly our Creator could use His Living Light to create us. I believe this may be what Jesus is also showing us by embedding a star-tetrahedron in his prayer.

When a laser is focused through a small piece of holographic film, the whole hologram appears, so each piece contains the whole hologram. This would explain why spiritual teachers, including Jesus, say *the kingdom of God is within you.* If the universe were a hologram, it would also explain how Jesus and the Ancient Ones were able to perform their miracles. Time travel wasn't accomplished by propelling themselves through space at the speed of light. It was a matter of going within and surrendering to the Light. I now believe this is exactly what we see Pacal and Chan Bahlam doing in the Sun Cross Codex. Surrendering to the Light!

This holographic theory even explained what Doris did and taught. By being compassionately present, she could feel another person within herself. By simply being fully present and genuine, by loving them as herself, she could assist in releasing their self-judgments, which were the cause of their disease. Albert Einstein's special theory of relativity ($E=mc^2$) is not about what happens when we accelerate to the speed of light but is really just the opposite. It's about what happens when we stop completely to come fully into the present where God is, who is The Light. I believe the holographic theory beautifully explains how *Thy Kingdome come, thy will be done* is describing how we awaken to our highest illumined nature.

THE RAPTURE

In Mexico, Hunbatz-Men told us that many of his insights had come directly from the Mayan storytellers whose job is to keep their ancient myths fresh and alive. These myths describe the Ancient Ones as gods having super-human abilities. Hunbatz said that the Ancient Ones predicted that, as we approach the year 2012, earth shall be bathed in new frequencies of light, and that these new frequencies were already subtly changing us in ways that we might not even notice. This wasn't hard for either Barbara or me to believe, as we were both very aware of how much our relationship with the prayer and our trip to Mexico had changed us, and how quickly.

In the early to mid-seventies, two scientists, Terrence L. McKenna and his brother Dennis, also predicted that, in the year 2012, human evolution would make a similar and unprecedented evolutionary leap. By programming a computer with all the significant historic developments of mankind, the McKenna brothers projected a graph of human evolution. It goes vertical around the year 2012. They asserted these findings:

A 4,300-year cycle from urbanization to the dawn of modern science,

A 368-year cycle when science realized more discoveries than in the whole previous 4,300-year cycle,

A 67-year cycle, from the technological breakthroughs of the 1940's to the peak in 2012, when there will be more acceleration than there was between the time of Galileo and Hiroshima,

A 384-day cycle in 2011-2012, when there will be more transformations than in all the previous cycles,

A six-day cycle, at the end of which things will move even faster,

until a grand climax, in which they predict "in the last 135 minutes, 18

barriers, comparable to the appearance of life on earth, the invention

of language, or the achievement of immortality, will be crossed, 13

of them in the last .0075 of a second."

Talk about fast!

There is a correlation between many different sources that lead to these same conclusions. In Durango, we met a Seventh Day Adventist minister who was an expert in the chronology of the Bible. He didn't know a thing about the Mayans, but as he wrote the apocalyptic time frames in the Bible on the blackboard, we were amazed. They matched those of the Mayan Calendar exactly. The evolutionary leap, which both the Mayas and the McKenna's foretell, is perfectly described in the Bible as the "rapture". In I Corinthians 15:51-52, we hear *we shall all be changed, in a moment, in the twinkling of an eye.*

ANTS ON A LOG

Not long ago, I saw a documentary in which an astronomer was tracking our solar systems journey through the Milky Way. He said that our sun would align with the center of the Milky Way. Guess when? 2012! This reminded me of something else Hunbatz- Men said. "Our sun's rotation has been far from the galactic center, and this has made spiritual evolution on earth slow and challenging. But," he continued, "soon our sun will become the central sun of the Milky Way. Then, Hunab Ku, "God of the central sun," or God, will reside within our sun, and our solar system will be transformed into a heaven, the Eighth Heaven.

Science is presenting us with other facts that support what Hunbatz-Men said. For example, earth's background, base frequency, or "heartbeat" (called Schumann Resonance, or SR) is now rising dramatically, and they don't know why. For decades, the overall measurement of 7.8 cycles per second was so constant, that global military communications were developed on this frequency. Recent reports, however, set the rate at over 11 cycles and climbing, and again they don't know why. At the same time, earth's magnetic field is decreasing, and they can't explain that, either. As I hear more and more things like this, I remember what my friend Eldon used to say: "We are like ants on a log floating down a river. We're trying so hard to control what happens on this log (earth), that we don't see where our log is headed." What the Mayas and biblical prophets obviously have in common is a great interest in where our log is headed.

THE PRODIGAL SON
In the Gospel of Luke, Jesus tells the story of a man who has two sons. The younger demands his share of his inheritance while his father is still living and goes off

to a distant country where he *wastes his substance with riotous living*. He eventually must take work as a swine herder. When he comes to his senses, he decides to return home and throw himself on his father's mercy. However, instead of being punished or chastised as he expects, his father greets him with open arms. His father hardly gives him a chance to apologize and then kills a fatted calf to celebrate his son's return.

I see our human story unfolding much like the parable of the prodigal son. I think our Western world is a lot like the younger son who left his father's house to live riotously. Our Western world is notoriously wasteful of the resources Our Father has given us. I see the older son who stayed at home much like the indigenous people of the earth. They have remained close to Our Father by living simply and in harmony with the laws of nature. The return of the younger son to live again with his father is very similar to the unprecedented spiritual revival that is currently taking place.

The Lord's Prayer is also like this parable. In it, we descend from Our Father in heaven into temptation in order to be delivered from evil. What the McKenna brothers computed was the same journey of our western world: from hunters and gatherers to farmers, to industrialists, to a high-tech culture, and finally to this information age and beyond. What they see happening very soon is an evolutionary leap. What could cause that? It sounds like deliverance to me. When I ask how we will be delivered, I see that we must simply let go.

PLEASURE ANXIETY

Surrendering to the present is what made Doris so effective. She didn't call it love, but that's what it felt like.

There is a great misconception that love is something we can do, but it's not. Love is who we are. In order to be loving, we must simply let go and be ourselves. The problem is that we are so busy being what we think we need to be, that we don't really know ourselves. When I see videos of Mother Teresa's healing ministry, I'm surprised at how much she reminds me of Doris. I'm surprised, because they were so different. Mother Teresa was devoutly religious, and Doris was very anti-religion.

What Doris and Mother Teresa did, also seems quite different? Mother Teresa helped people who were dying in the streets of Calcutta. Doris helped people in Los Angeles who just wanted to feel better. Mother Teresa did it for the glory of God, and Doris did it just because it felt good. They were as different as Christianity and Yoga. And, like Yoga and Christianity, they were both dedicated to fulfilling real needs - which, by definition, is loving. They were not so different, after all. When we're in need and nothing else matters, then we let go of everything else, and this is when we experience our personal miracles.

Both Doris and Mother Teresa were part of peoples' personal miracles, as they were both dedicated to something that was needed. In my work with the game, I have often been blessed to be part of someone's personal miracle. That's what the game does - it identifies what we need. How it does this reminds me of what Jesus said. *Man does not live by bread alone, but by every word from the mouth of God.* The game offers us the bit of spiritual encouragement we need to be all that we can be right now. Within every need is this one: to simply be and live as God's children.

Our needs humble us, but pleasure does, too. These two are as seemingly different as Doris and Mother Teresa, but we respond to pleasure and fear very similarly. Both fear and pleasure are disarming. Both cause us to let go, to be present, and to feel vulnerable; both need and pleasure inspire fear. The fear of pleasure is called "pleasure anxiety," and is important to acknowledge, because saying the Lord's Prayer correctly is a deeply pleasurable experience. Pray means "to ask." Jesus said, "Ask and you shall receive," and receiving what we need is a very pleasurable experience indeed.

Have you heard these bits of advice to "eat the peach" and "smell the roses?" Both encourage us to be present and enjoy the beautiful deliciousness of our lives. I believe that's what Our Father wants us to do; but when we do, our false, ego identities often experience both fear and guilt. Much of our lives are spent wanting what we don't have but when we finally get it, we often find that we are not prepared. Knowing that Our Father wants us to be happy expands our capacity for pleasure more than any other thing I know of.

FAITH

Milton beautifully described an ego's point of view when he said, "It is better to reign in hell, than to serve in heaven." The question is, what could possibly make living in hell better than living in heaven? The answer is, our fear of death. Here is a good example of how the simplest and purest truths are distorted. Most of us were taught that we go to heaven when we die, and it's true. In order to come into the present, into God's kingdom that is *at hand,* we must go through what has often been described as "ego death." The Bible tells us that our human journey began when Adam and Eve ate the fruit of "knowledge of good and evil." This knowledge is what our egos use to *judge* what is right, wrong, better, worse, good and bad, and so on.

This knowledge of good and evil is what we use to create the laws of our societies that ultimately define what we believe and create. If, for a moment, you will pay attention to your own thinking process, what you will observe is your ego mind endlessly evaluating everything and everyone of any importance to you. What we see in the Lord's Prayer are the experiences that activate our mind most of all: daily bread, forgiveness (betrayal), and temptation. That's because a primary function of this prayer is to put our minds to rest so that we can simply be present, in heaven.

Our egos identify themselves by what they do and accomplish, including all these activities of determining what is good, bad, right or wrong, etc. Without all of that, the ego begins losing its strength; and this experience of being diminished feels like death. What the Lord's Prayer is designed to do is move our awareness of ourselves as primarily physical beings (the cube) to the spiritual inner awareness of being, *the light of the world* (the star).

The way back to paradise is expressed in the Lord's Prayer as *Thy kingdom come, thy will be done.* God's will is the ultimate light called love and doing God's will is just being present. Love doesn't *judge* anything, so in love our egos don't have much to do. That's okay; the tail has been wagging the dog, I mean the god, long enough! To have heavenly lives, we must train our minds to let go and get out of our way. What prevents us from "eating the peach," "smelling the roses," or from enjoying anything is thinking! *As you think in your heart you shall become,* so thinking in ways you want to feel is a great way to use your mind. How to do this in the most balanced and effective way is what we have found in the Lord's Prayer.

Pleasure anxiety is just another name for the ego death that we all experience as we walk the "middle path" and approach the "narrow gate." Falling in love is another name for this. When we fall, we lose control, and this is part of what we all must experience as we enter into the kingdom of love that is at hand. Jesus tells us that it is harder for a rich man to enter heaven than for a camel to pass through the eye of the needle. Why? Because rich men generally have the biggest egos and are the most attached to being in control. What enables us to keep letting go even when we are terrified is faith. Faith is the seed of the promise that the Lord's Prayer is designed to nurture and grow. Faith is the key.

Part VI
"THE BLESSINGS ALREADY ARE"

THE THIRD RIDDLE

The third riddle with which Jesus prepares us to receive his prayer is my favorite. Just before he taught this prayer, he said, "*Your Father knows what you need before you ask Him. Therefore, pray in this manner: Our Father who art in heaven....*" The word pray means "to ask," but if God *knows what we need before we ask Him*, why ask? Why pray? Obviously, our prayers are not to inform God but to evolve our own faith in his ever-present love for us. It is as Mother Teresa said, *"Prayer enlarges the heart until it is capable of containing God's gift of Himself* (Love)."

THE ULTIMATE POSITIVE THOUGHT

I was thirty-three when our magical journey began with this question, *"What do you want?"* My answer was simple; I just wanted "to be a good father." Up to that moment, I had been working very hard to be just that. Back then, I believed that I needed lots of money to be a good dad; but each time I came close to making it, something unexpected would happen. On one occasion, the liability insurance for one of my inventions jumped from $50,000 a year to over $500,000, so everything came to a grinding halt. Another time, we were finalizing a deal for a game I'd invented when Sears, our only customer, showed no profit to its shareholders for its first time ever. Consequently, all new products, my game included, were frozen immediately and indefinitely.

Losing Progressive Fitness and the Total Trainer felt like "strike three" to me. When that happened, it seemed to me that God Himself was blocking my way. In a way, I think He was. It wasn't that He was punishing me or keeping me from succeeding. In fact, it was just the opposite. I had been compromising my own happiness to make money, because deep down inside I believed that's what a good husband and father had to do. That's what my dad had done. Furthermore, I was in business with people that I really didn't like.

It wasn't working, because I was wrong. How it does work is to *follow your heart, and everything you need will be provided for you perfectly and effortlessly.* That's just another way of saying *Seek first the kingdom of God (happiness) and all these things (what we truly need) shall be added unto you.* That evening, I realized that what I wanted from my dad was permission to follow my heart. The best way he could have given me that was through his example, and the best way to give this ultimate gift to my own children was through my example. Once I had accepted this, I was faced with another question: *If you had all the money you could ever need or want, what would you do?*

"*The greatest treason is to do the right thing for the wrong reason.*"

T. S. Eliot

Money is not what any of us really wants. It is what we believe we need to get what we really want. I had to rise above this pervasive lie to begin pursuing my heart's passion, and so will you. If you are thinking that you need certain things or conditions to be happy, then your heart is going to believe that happiness is hard to come by; and that is the real lie. You can make yourself happy right now by just imagining that you are doing what you love to do. You can, because *as you think in your heart you shall become.* Once our heart realizes that we are guiding it to happiness, we quickly gain its trust and cooperation. Thinking unhappy thoughts, on the other hand, closes or hardens our heart.

The Lord's Prayer is more than a happy thought. It is a sequence of eight affirmations that illuminates the happiest of all thoughts--the potential for us all to experience unconditional love or heaven on earth. Why is this the ultimate happy or positive thought? Why is this thought more productive than holding any other one? It's what makes the Lord's Prayer such a powerful spiritual instrument. It is not just true; it is both the highest and truest aspiration of mankind, and it is God's will. Affirming that we are Our Father's children unites our will with His. There is nothing more powerful, positive, or productive than that, as expressed in *thy kingdom come thy will be done.*

THE LORD GIVES

Right away, pursuing the promise of the Lord's Prayer began making us happier and more productive. In every way, our lives were definitely more magical. At first, we both still had jobs, we were still broke, and our credit was still terrible; but none of that seemed to matter. It wasn't just that it didn't bother us; it really didn't matter. There were no thunderclaps or brilliant flashes. As things began to change, we hardly noticed. First, we got better jobs and had more time to enjoy our children and each other. When Barbara was eight months pregnant with our seventh child, Shawn, the rent-controlled home we'd been renting for nine years was sold. Then the group of Beverly Hills lawyers who'd bought it for an investment evicted us. We were shaken but trusted that we were being loved.

Finding an affordable place for a family of nine in Los Angeles isn't easy and dealing with this ruthless law firm shouldn't have been easy-but for us it was. The same day that we got our eviction notice, I showed it to one of my customers at work. He was also a lawyer, and he just happened to know the law firm that was evicting us. He also didn't like them much and offered to help us make them back off, for free. Soon Barbara found and fell in love with a much nicer home, but we couldn't afford it. Then the realtor handling it called back and said they would lower the rent for us. It had fifteen-foot ceilings, two fireplaces, and a Jacuzzi in the master bath. Best of all, it was just three blocks from Venice Beach and very close to the Santa Monica Pier, where we both worked. In short, all of this was much better than anything we could have imagined. We had been guided and blessed.

Four months later, our dream house in Venice also went up for sale. Instead of being evicted, however, our next-door neighbors, whom we barely knew, offered to loan us the money to buy it. We were stunned and very grateful. Shortly after that, Barbara was offered the management contract for the Hippodrome building that housed the Carousel on the Santa Monica Pier, and a gift shop concession was part of the deal. Two years later, in 1989, not long after both Barbara and I had gotten new cars and taken our trip to Mexico, we sold our beautiful four-bedroom house in Venice Beach. That enabled us to pay cash for a six-bedroom home in Durango, Colorado that had awesome views and miles of national forest just outside our front door.

With no mortgage and enough money in the bank, we took a whole year off, looking for options and deciding what was next. Barbara and I were both spinning as the whirlwind of blessings were being showered upon us. I took the Flower of Life workshop twice in 1989, as well as an intensive hypnosis workshop. Both offered us much deeper understandings of our work with the Lord's Prayer and The Game. Soon I was teaching, lecturing, and playing The Game full time. In addition to the Lord's Prayer, our progress between 1982-1989 was facilitated by this truth, *Freedom is having nothing left to lose.* Soon, however, we would realize how just the opposite can also be true.

"When you are in a state of nonacceptance, it's difficult to learn. A clenched fist cannot receive a gift, and a clenched psyche grasped tightly against the reality of what must not be accepted cannot easily receive a lesson".

John Roger

HEREDITY

I had just begun to wonder how we could hold on to all these wonderful blessings, when my father and mother decided to visit us in Durango. My mom was confined to a wheelchair. Early one morning in 1973, my parent's dreams were decimated when an operation to fix an aneurysm in Mom's brain left her almost completely paralyzed. When Mom's pride made her resistant to rehabilitation, Dad indulged her. Then they were both permanently crippled by her condition and by their decision.

Two weeks before mom discovered this aneurysm, she was going through some kind of midlife crisis, and, for the first time ever, she began reaching out to me. It seemed so ironic that I, the great disappointment of her life, would be the one that she could talk to, but I was, and that felt so good. Mom said that she was having doubts about everything - her marriage to Dad, her relationship with her mother, my "Nana," and with the church. We talked for hours as she let out thoughts, feelings, and fears that she had been suppressing for so many years. We had just begun talking about what her choices were, when she suddenly stopped calling.

One morning about two weeks later, Nana called and told me what had happened to Mom the morning after our last conversation. No one knew that Mom and I had been talking. As all their relationships with me had been so challenging, Dad and Nana decided not to tell me until all the decisions had been made. The decisions they made, and kept making, were terrible, in my opinion. Consequently, my mom remained literally trapped within her own body for the next thirty years. As they suspected I would, I adamantly disagreed with their choices. I don't know that I could have done any better, but Dad and Nana never asked, and were very offended when I could not keep my opinions to myself. Fortunately, I was in therapy with Doris at the time and had plenty of opportunities to vent, reflect, and share my feelings with my other family in Los Angeles.

I now realize that my dad really did follow his heart, but his heart was broken at least three times. The first time was in the war that he never talked about (WWII). He flew twenty-seven bombing missions as a bottom turret gunner. That was the most dangerous position on a B17, and he chose it so no one else would have to. Dad was decorated several times for bravery and for going beyond the call of duty. He received a Purple Heart when a piece of shrapnel from anti-aircraft fire ripped through his flight jacket, and he was wounded. I learned all of this from my grandmother, but Dad himself never spoke a word about it. I believe Dad lost his faith in God in the skies somewhere over Germany, and he never said anything about that, either.

I was the one who broke his heart the second time. He provided me with all the opportunities to become what he knew I could be. The problem was, I didn't want to become a doctor. As I became more and more rebellious, it was obvious that Dad felt betrayed and bewildered - not just by me, but also by life itself. When Mom became ill, Dad's scarred heart was broken again, and a year and a half later, he had his first open-heart surgery. Dad wasn't bitter; he was hurt. He thought he'd done all that he could to create a good life. He'd sacrificed and saved, had married the girl that he loved, had been moral and responsible. The only way he could make any sense of it was that it was his bad luck.

Nearly every conversation Dad and I had after Mom's operation ended with his crying. We only spoke a few times a year. When every single conversation ends with pain, after a while you have to ask, what's the point? But when Dad called to say that they were coming to Durango, an old dream was revived. This would be my opportunity to finally show them both what I had accomplished, and on my own terms. Financial security was most important to my dad, but it had not played any part in my decision to embrace the Lord's Prayer. I didn't know it at the time; but somehow, in the process of trying to impress my dad in this way, I lost touch with our Heavenly Father.

When Mom and Dad arrived and entered our beautiful new home for the first time, my dad was unusually quiet. As he looked around at all the space and the view, I could see that he was impressed. He asked me how much the payments were, but I'd already told him that we paid cash for it. When I reminded him, he seemed bewildered, and I imagined that he was trying to reconcile how I could have gone from being broke to having such financial security so quickly. How does a forty-year-old waiter do that? He didn't say so, but I'm almost certain he wondered if I was dealing drugs again.

The whole time my mom and dad were there, he seemed more concerned than impressed or happy for me. On several occasions, I felt as though he wanted to say something to me but couldn't. He'd never given me a complement or congratulations in forty years, but I was certain that this was what he was working up to. Finally, on their last day in Durango, just as they were preparing to leave, my dad took me aside. "Son, I don't understand how or why you've been so lucky, but I know that luck doesn't last. If you will work hard and be practical, then you may be able to keep all of this." His parting words voiced my own concerns, and from then on, I was consumed with holding on to what we had.

Looking back now, I see how powerful the imprints and influences that we receive from our earthly parents truly are. I also realize how confining they can be. Can we ever rise above the powerful influences of heredity? I believe we can by embracing Our Heavenly Father's will. This, however, is a life-long process; and the influences of our parents will always be a key part of who we are, how we learn, and what defines our unique expressions.

SPINNING

I now realize that my mom and dad's visit had such an influence on me because I was already very concerned about holding on to what we had. It's just one more example of how Our Father's law works. We attract what we believe, and at that moment I believed exactly what my dad said. I am still amazed at how the results of our spiritual quest could have blinded us to their source, but that is what happened. The Lord's Prayer transformed our lives both subtly and magnificently. At first, everything seemed so natural and ordinary, and then later, we were completely distracted by the wondrous results. We were so busy reacting to what was happening, that we never took the time to connect the dots and realize the role the Lord's Prayer had played in our good fortune. It wasn't until we let go and again had nothing much to lose that we could see what really happened.

Lots of people would say that what did happen is a perfect example of how "the Lord gives and the Lord taketh away," but I don't believe that, at all. I believe God's law allows each of us to attract what we believe. What we had come here by letting go, so by trying to hold on, we naturally stopped the flow. It was as if we swam from the shallow end of the pool into the deep end, and then tried to stand up. When we realized that we were in over our heads, our fears of drowning prevented us from realizing that we swam there ourselves. We arrived in Durango in a state of euphoria, enchanted by our recent experiences with The Game and the Ancient Ones. These, together with our newfound financial freedom, our spacious new home, new friends, and the praise and appreciation of our new clients uplifted by our work had our heads and hearts spinning.

Spinning is what spirituality is all about. The English word spiritual comes from the Latin word "spiritus" meaning "breath." Like everything in Our Lord's spinning universe, our breath moves in a spiral as it

130

flows through us. A star-tetrahedron also spins. Everything that is not attached or resistant naturally spins as fast as its state of balance will allow, our own consciousness included. The faster we spin, the brighter our light or aura grows, and the more we let go, the more balanced we become, the faster we spin. Everything leading up to Durango had moved Barbara and me into a more complete state of letting go. That's how God works; as long as we are alive, there is always more to let go of. The Lord's Prayer presents us with eight different ways or levels of letting go; or surrendering to Our Father's will. The forces of our spinning spirits naturally drew our blessings to us. That's how *Seek first the kingdom of God and all these things shall be added unto us* works. But when you are spinning fast and trying to hold on, what happens? That's exactly what we were about to learn.

CRASHING

Once I began to fear losing what we had, it was like riding one of those giant Brahma bulls in the rodeo. But Spirit is no bull. Trying to hold on just pulled us out of our centers even more. Before my parents ever arrived, Barbara and I were taking some practical steps to insure our financial security. Soon after they left, we began reviving an old dream, Barbara's Café. There's another important lesson. Spinning faster is a bit like driving fast on a mountain road. It is very important to keep your eyes on the road and not look back. Before the doors of Barbara's Café were open, our old dream of owning our own 50's-style café had already become a nightmare. Everything, from the jukebox to the ice-cream soda fountain cost more than we'd imagined, and by the end of 1990, we'd mortgaged our beautiful home to the hilt.

Our home was threatened with foreclosure five times in 1991. Just keeping our children properly fed and warm, and the doors of the café open through that winter was a real struggle. Barbara was working sixteen hours a day in the café, while I worked as a truck driver by day and a waiter at night. Every cent we made went to pay our employees, rent, utilities, and supplies. We still had to borrow from friends, family, and even our own kids to make ends meet, but the ends never did meet, and we continually fell farther and farther behind. While Barb and I struggled through that first long winter in hopes that the summer tourist season would save us, our oldest daughters were looking after our youngest children, so they were stressed, too. I couldn't even count the number of times during the next year and a half that our phone and utilities at home were cut off. At one point, we were getting so many phone calls from bill collectors that it was a relief to have no phone. Having no electricity was harder to deal with.

A CONSPIRACY?

There was a brief, hopeful moment early that summer, when the flood of tourists was upon us. As we were holding our collective breath and hoping to make enough to start paying off our giant debt, we heard that the Disney movie "Peter Pan" was coming to Durango's only theater. Barbara and I began sharing our childhood memories of Peter Pan with each other, much as we had with the Lord's Prayer eight years earlier. We saw this as an opportunity to share Peter's magical oath and Tinker Bell's healing with our children as a delightful relief, and even a good omen. Waiting for our kids to meet Peter Pan and Tinker Bell was a bit like waiting for Christmas, for us. When the movie finally arrived, we took the whole family to a Sunday matinee. Anticipating a truly religious experience, we splurged on candy, popcorn, and sodas for everyone. As the movie began, our hearts were pounding. Would Peter's magic touch them as it had us when we were kids? Would this experience contribute to their spiritual development as it had ours? As I watched their faces out of the corner of my eye, I realized how difficult adulthood must have looked to them at that moment. I felt responsible for that, which made sharing Peter's magic with them even more important.

BARBARA: When the movie was over, I was still waiting. Surely, I couldn't have slept through the audience's taking the oath to "never grow up," or them all clapping to heal Tinker Bell. Bodie and I walked out silently together behind the children. They had no idea what they'd just missed, but I felt stunned and betrayed. That original movie was so beautiful. It was an important part of my own personal life development. I just couldn't imagine how they could, or why they would remove the most magical heartfelt parts of it. It just didn't make sense. I felt disoriented and off balance.

Once we were outside, as we were adjusting to the bright mid-day sunlight, I asked Bodie, "What happened?" He looked stunned, too, and answered, "I don't know. I don't understand. Why would they remove the best parts of such a wonderful movie?" Bodie held me as I started to cry. I told the kids that it was because I was so happy that we all got to see the movie together, but I was really feeling like there was something truly wrong with our world. I always do my best to look at the positive side of things, but at that moment I just couldn't see anything bright or good. Standing there, with my family all around me, in one of the most beautiful towns on earth, I should have been in bliss; but I wasn't. I was consumed with the sense of a dark conspiracy designed to deprive us of all our dreams. Later that night, when the kids were finally asleep, Bodie and I cried in each other's arms and assured each other that everything would be okay.

A REALLY EXPENSIVE CUP OF COFFEE

BODIE: The tourist season lasted about three weeks. We paid our bills on time that month, but that was it. Barbara was determined that we would survive, but I was certain that we could not stand another winter like the last one. One morning, on my way to my truck-driving job, I stopped as usual at Barbara's Café to be sure that the cook showed up and that he had everything he would need for the breakfast crowd. It was difficult for me to get there during business hours, but early, before we were open, I always enjoyed beginning my long day with a cup of our delicious coffee.

That morning, I was sipping a little slower than usual. I watched as white steam slowly rose off the black surface of my second cup, and I heard my inner voice say, "That's a really expensive cup of coffee." I remembered my friend, Gilo, saying, "So Bodie, you spent a lot of time and money and worked really hard to create really hard jobs for yourselves?" I didn't like hearing that because it was so true. As I stared at the steam rising off my coffee that morning, I realized that we'd stopped enjoying our beautiful life and surroundings and had forgotten the magical journey that brought us to this heavenly place. As

I continued sipping that "really expensive cup of coffee." I could feel myself letting go. After having a really good laugh about the absurdity of it, I felt better. A few days later, we closed Barbara's Café. Then we held each other and cried again before turning to face our fears of the unknown that we'd struggled so hard to avoid.

THE BLESSINGS ALREADY ARE

In just two and a half years, Barbara and I had gone from thriving to barely surviving. When we finally swallowed our pride to accept food stamps and charity from strangers, things started getting better. We were afraid of what would happen if we couldn't afford to properly feed and shelter our children, but we could only take one day at a time. I believe that's what *Give us this day our daily bread* is about. We had no money and a huge debt, but we were still together, with a beautiful family, and in good health. Our family had obviously grown stronger, wiser, and closer; and we knew we were being blessed when our house sold one day before the final foreclosure auction. We even made enough profit to rent a small farm in Bondad, just outside of Durango, while deciding what to do next.

As I write about this now, I am reminded of what Jesus had said about the house that was built upon a rock:

"Therefore whosoever heareth these sayings of mine, and doeth them, I will liken him unto a wise man, which built his house upon a rock: And the rain descended, and the floods came, and the winds blew, and beat upon that house; and it fell not: for it was founded upon a rock. And everyone that heareth these sayings of mine, and doeth them not, shall be likened unto a foolish man, which built his house upon the sand: And the rain

descended, and the floods came, and the winds blew, and beat upon that house; and it fell: and great was the fall of it." (Matthew 7:24-29)

We got our beautiful house, but there was obviously no rock beneath it. If we were to avoid repeating these lessons in the future, we had to find that rock, and that's when I began praying again. As I did, my favorite teacher, John Roger, began appearing in my thoughts. Each time, he said the same thing. It was something I often heard him say: *The blessings already are*. Now, for the first time, I understood how very logical this statement was. If God is loving, all-powerful, and ever-present, as the Holy Scriptures proclaim, then the only possible explanation for *everything* that happens must be *the blessings already are*. In other words, no matter what happens, we as God's children are being loved. If everything that we went through and let go of in Durango was the price of finding this "rock," it was well worth it. Affirming that *the blessings already are* always brings me strength, stability, clarity, and hope, no matter what is happening.

OUR LIVES ARE EXPERIMENTS

After the Flower of Life workshop, and before I was consumed by my fears and the café, I had time to read during those first blissful months. I became fascinated by how quantum physicists were concluding, from their experiments, what spiritual teachers have been saying for ages--that what we think and believe defines our realities. It was during this time that I read *The Holographic Universe*, and when Shawn Michael so eloquently informed me, "Jesus is fast." I learned that the pioneers of this belief, Albert Einstein and David Bohm, both had worked on the Manhattan Project developing the first atomic bombs during World War II. In later life, they were both haunted by the consequences of their actions, which compelled them to reach a higher understanding of life.

Bohm said, *"So one begins to wonder what is going to happen to the human race. Technology keeps on advancing with greater and greater power, either for good or for destruction."* He goes on to ask, *"What is the source of all this trouble? I'm saying that the source is basically in thought. Many people would think that such a statement is crazy, because thought is the one thing we have with which to solve our problems. That's part of our tradition. Yet it looks as if the thing we use to solve our problems with is the source of our problems. It's like going to the doctor and having him make you ill."*

My interests in Albert Einstein and David Bohm were rekindled shortly after we let go of Barbara's Café, and they helped me to see how each human life is an experiment. Viewing my own exploded life as the dust was settling, I realized how *the blessings already are* enabled me to take responsibility for the failure of my experiment. Again, this is what I believe *Give us this day our daily bread* really means. Accepting responsibility for the bomb I had baked enabled me to learn from my mistakes very quickly. *The blessings already are* made my life so simple. If I could create all of that and let it go, then certainly I could create something better and more lasting. With this in mind, the next leg of our adventure began.

"I want to know God's thoughts; the rest are details."
                                     Albert Einstein

Thinking of my life as an experiment reminded me that, as God's child, my job is to learn and grow and have fun. This simple thought enabled me to forgive myself for all the suffering I still believed was my fault, so that I could get on with the next experiment. I also realized how important it was that my next experiment be devoted to proving that *the blessings already are*, and I saw how this premise aligns with the idea that *the kingdom of God is at hand*. You could even say that the purpose of the Lord's Prayer is to prepare our hearts and minds for harvesting the blessings that already are.

"Self-forgiveness is the key to the kingdom. It not only opens the door, it's the hinges on the door, it's the key to the door, and it's also the little bell that rings and lets you know the door opened."

John Roger

As Barbara and I began moving forward with this new clarity and focus, the magic was immediately apparent. While Barb and the kids enjoyed a well-deserved summer of fun on our little farm, I responded to three invitations to come and share our game. Two of these were in California, and the third was an invitation from our friend Mary in Atlanta, Georgia. The game and I were well received on all three trips, but the magic that happened in Atlanta and when Mary took me to North Carolina made it crystal clear where our family would be headed next. In August of 1992, Barbara and I relocated our family from the Rocky Mountains of Colorado to the Smoky Mountains of Western North Carolina. Our faith was growing, and we were once again living in the moment.

LIFE IN THE BUCKLE

Even before leaving for North Carolina, Barbara and I were learning how to apply the magic of *the blessings already are* to our lives with great success. Four days before we were ready to make this move, we got a call from Barbara Henderson, the realtor who had found us a house to rent in Waynesville, NC. She said that the owners were having second thoughts about renting their house to a family with so many children. Since she'd looked everywhere and could find nothing else large enough for all of us, she suggested that we wait a couple of months and move there after the tourist season, when more homes would be available. But waiting was not an option.

Not only was our household packed up, we were also financially committed. Since we had no credit, we already had paid cash to reserve two trucks. We also paid cash to reserve three hotel rooms in the six places where we would be spending the night along the way. Not only that, in two more months the small profit we had made on the house would be gone, and we would not be able to move anywhere. After six days on the road, we arrived with our two large trucks and three cars in Waynesville. Barbara Henderson still had not found us a place to live, and my Barbara and I calculated that our family had just enough money to last two more weeks of living in motels and eating in restaurants.

Early the next morning, we got a call from Barbara Henderson. She asked us to meet her in front of the post office, which we did, and right across the street was a beautiful house with a "for rent" sign. Barbara's secretary had seen them putting up the sign on her way to work, and that was our first home in North Carolina. Not only was it much larger than the other house, it was half the price and in a much better location. In addition, there was a garage apartment in the back where I could work privately playing The Game with new clients. You could say that we were starting over, but in many ways, Waynesville was much better for us. Had we not been forced to sell our house in Durango, it is doubtful that we would have ever moved. Fortunately, as we'd hoped, there in the "buckle of the Bible belt" our game was well received. Within just a few months, it was practically supporting the financial needs of our large family.

DADDY, I REALLY WANT A HORSE

Here is another story about how *the blessings already are* resulted in another kind of miracle. It was a spring afternoon during our third year in North Carolina. Our whole family was helping some new friends, who were living on a small farm, to plant their vegetable garden. Afterwards, our ten-year-old daughter, Jessica, asked me to take a walk with her up to the upper pasture where some horses were grazing. As we stood admiring them, Jessica said with a twinkle in her eyes, "Daddy, I really, really want a horse."

My body began tightening and I felt guilty that I couldn't say, "Sure, what kind do you want?" I also couldn't tell my ten-year-old daughter with twinkling eyes that we couldn't even afford to keep a horse, let alone buy one. Instead of telling Jessica the challenging facts of our financial circumstances, I said, "Jessie, I would also love for you to have a horse, so let's say a prayer together right now and ask God to help us with this." Then we held hands and I said, "Lord, we would love for Jessica to have her own beautiful, strong, and healthy horse. We ask now for this, or something better, for her highest good." Then we said the Lord's Prayer together, and I assured Jessica that it was in God's hands, and that, whatever happened, we would know it was for the best. The point I want to make here is that my new belief in *the blessings already are,* enabled me to respond to Jessica in this positive way, even though my emotions were responding negatively to her "unreasonable" request.

Not long after that, Barbara received a call from our friend Lois. She knew that Jessica was choosing to home school that year, so she asked if Jessica would like a part- time job working at a nearby horse stable. Naturally, Jessie said she would, and her job entailed feeding and riding the horses to exercise them. Obviously, Jessie was thrilled, and a few years later she actually got her own horse, "Dandy." Jessie assisted at his birth, and she broke and trained him herself; so, their bond is uniquely true and strong. Of all the people I have ever met who have been blessed to have their own horse, none of them has such a deep and mutually rewarding relationship as Dandy and Jessica do.

TWO CARS AND SOME SOCKS

About six months before Jessica experienced her horse miracle, both of our family cars broke down within a couple of months of each other. Most of my work was in Atlanta Georgia, and Raleigh and Highlands, North Carolina. We encouraged our clients to come to us, but the two-and-a-half to five-and-a-half-hour drive was too much for most of them. In many ways, we were even more financially challenged than in Durango, but we were handling it much better.

After Jessica got her job at the stables, she and I had several occasions to acknowledge and discuss how and why our prayer that day was answered. After one of our conversations, Jessica asked me, "Daddy, if we had lots of money, what would you buy?" At that time, we didn't even own a car, so I answered, "I would buy a car for your mom and one for myself." Then I added, "And I would also get myself some new socks." Then Jessica suggested that we pray about it, as we did for her horse. Within less than a week, we were given a nice car; and three days later, we were given another one. The second car wasn't quite as nice. But when I went to pick it up, Miriam, our benefactor, said, "Oh Bodie, there's a bag of new socks on the back seat. If you don't want them, please just give them to the Goodwill." Ask and you shall receive!

Over the next several years, Barbara drove her car well over one hundred thousand miles. My car, however, had some problems that we couldn't afford to fix, so we let it go. A while later, I prayed again for a car; and again, in less than a week, we were given one. Before I could really enjoy it, however, our newest driver, Ampara, wrecked it. She wasn't hurt, but the car was totaled; and I was beginning to wonder if I had "bad car-ma." When I prayed about this, my inner voice asked me that question again, "What do you want?" Obviously, I wanted a car, but there was something that I wanted more. I wanted to write a book that would enable me to share my passion for the Lord's Prayer and The Game with many more people.

As you know, in school I was a poor student, and English was my worst subject. What I really needed was the time to learn how to do this, as well as the discipline to show up, sit down, and get to work, day after day. That's what it takes, and for someone like me, this has taken a lot of time and patience. As I was realizing this, I also saw that having a car was a big distraction for me. Then I understood, God wasn't depriving me of a car, He was helping me by eliminating all the distracting things I would be doing if I had one.

CROSSES AND PEARLS

One day, shortly after our move to North Carolina, I was walking a new client from my office to her car, when I noticed our two youngest daughters watching me. As the client drove away, the girls approached. Jessica, who was nine and the older of the two, asked, "Daddy what do you do?" I smiled. Our new neighbors were obviously quizzing them, as small-town neighbors often do. Inventing new ways of describing my work with The Game was, and is, an ongoing task. Before I could create an appropriate response, Gabrielle, who was just seven, stepped up. She planted her little fist on her hip and, in a rather bossy, yet princess style, said, "Don't you know? He makes people cry."

Naturally I laughed. It was funny, but it was also one of those truth gems that come from the mouths of children. My last client had been crying. My private clients often did at some point during our game. It illuminates what Jesus called our "cross", and it shows us how to "pick up our cross" and use it for making our lives better. This cross is what makes us special and unique, and that's also why it causes us pain. What makes us special makes us different, which in turn stimulates our core fears of being separate and alone. That's why most of us avoid our cross at all costs, but in so doing we also avoid knowing and being the people, we truly are. Picking up our cross is being true to ourselves, and the rewards are realizing how God expresses His love through us and knowing the special gifts we have to offer. This is how this game help those who are willing to pick up their cross, but it takes great courage and determination to do this.

In helping people to understand the importance of this cross, I am often reminded of Jesus' parable of the Pearl of Great Price.

Again, the kingdom of heaven is like unto a merchantman, seeking goodly pearls: Who, when he had found one pearl of great price, went and sold all that he had, and bought it (Matthew 13:45-46).

I am also reminded of how the gates of heaven, The New Jerusalem, are also "twelve pearls." The way a pearl begins with a grain of sand, and how the oyster, deep beneath the surface, transforms it into a beautiful and valuable gift, is so descriptive of what The Game does and reveals. Our cross is like the grain of sand. Picking it up is meeting our challenges, and following Christ is transforming our challenges into beautiful pearls, or gifts.

I was taught that when Jesus said, "*Pick up your cross and follow me,*" he was telling us to bear the suffering of our life's challenges, but today I don't believe that. What I see, instead, is how he took the greatest challenges I can imagine and used them to express his most beautiful faith in the goodness of God. In doing this, he has inspired and lifted more and more human souls every day, for over two thousand years. That's some pearl.

The cross is often associated with trauma, but what is trauma? According to Wikipedia, "*A traumatic event involves a single experience, or an enduring or repeating event or events, that completely overwhelm the individual's ability to cope or integrate the ideas and emotions involved with that experience.*" Right there in that definition is the true power of the cross. When we are *completely overwhelmed,* our ego is humbled, as its agenda to be in control is overcome. So, in this place where we are traumatized, we may surrender whole-heartedly and unconditionally to God's will, to Love. When we pick up our cross, we can truly say and mean, "Lord, this is what I need or want, this or something better for my highest good." It takes courage and determination to do this, and such courage and determination are what picking up our cross helps us to develop.

To begin this transformational process, we must first accept that *the blessings already are.* Now we may pick up our cross or challenge, not as a great burden, but as the seed of an unrealized blessing. I would even say that having this faith that *the blessings already are* is the Pearl of Great Price, and the number of pearls we may create with it is unlimited. I believe that each of us may claim this power to create something good and useful from every experience by exercising the wisdom of *the blessings already are.* We do this by simply giving thanks to God for everything.

LIVE THE PROMISE

Our greatest blessings are not what we have, but who we are. We are the Light, which seems primitive and dangerous when our agenda is control. The Light wakens us from our illusionary dreams and compels us to let go, and what makes our lives difficult is trying to hold on. The Light comes forth like flowers from barren ground after a freezing winter, filling the void within us. We hide from the Light within us, but wise souls like Jesus and Buddha, Gandhi, and Mother Teresa continue to remind us that we are the Light and are capable of wondrous things.

Today, more than ever, people are restless, unsettled, and afraid, as they should be. We are approaching a new era, which is truly overwhelming. As we find ourselves unable to cope with this new reality, we will also realize many more opportunities to surrender our hearts in prayer. Naturally, we all desire a safe place to feel optimistic and hopeful, a place where we can rise above our fears to be the best people we can be. Such a place does exist, and Jesus described it in the Lord's Prayer when he said, *"Thy kingdom come, thy will be done, as is in heaven so also in earth."*

Jesus' prayer contains a sequence of eight spiritual exercises designed to lead us to this inner place of faith in, "The Promise" that we are always and everywhere being perfectly loved by everything. Now in Part VII, I will show you how simple it is to use His prayer and these eight spiritual exercises as creative tools. They move the mundane reality of our daily lives into the wondrous reality of this new era.

PART VII
"HEART DANCES"

IN JUST FOUR MINUTES

The treasures, which we have discovered during our journey with the Lord's Prayer, are a series of beautiful, heart-felt spiritual exercises that we call "Heart Dances". These uplifting and healing spiritual exercises, which come from the prayer, move our spiritual inner awareness through sequences of harmonic patterns. These patterns may be both felt and understood so like the prayer they also help to unify our thinking minds and our feeling hearts. While there are an infinite number of these Heart Dances™ there are eight basic ones and one "Master Dance."

Initially the eight basic Heart Dances™ came to us through our experiences with playing the game. It was about eleven years ago, while living in North Carolina that we realized how the insights that our game was revealing also had an entirely different but related purpose. That's when we began to realize how the game was actually made of these Heart Dances™. As we began experimenting with these Heart Dances™ we were amazed at how powerfully uplifting they were. Since then our focus has steadily moved from the importance of understanding towards the importance of "dancing" to the rhythms of our lives.

Over the past eleven years we have spent countless hours experimenting with and observing how these Heart Dances™ affect us. Our most crucial lesson about them is challenging to accept and difficult to practice. It is this: As Each of these Heart Dances™ illuminates a most eloquent understanding of our human nature the opportunity it presents is to suspend understanding and simply dance. What I love about dancing is how it liberates me from my normal analytical thinking processes. I think you will agree that thinking and dancing are incompatible and the same is true of these Heart Dances™.

For the sake of your curiosity and to help you better understand how our approach to the Lord's Prayer has come together, I will begin by offering a more specific understanding of how these Heart Dances™ have gradually come to us through our relationships with the seven chakras, seven branches of yoga, our characters, sacred patterns and of course the Lord's Prayer over these past twenty-five years. My descriptions of them will be condensed so you may want to read each one over several times. In the end however, to know these Heart Dances™ you will need to suspend your desire to understand in order to dance to them.

Our ultimate goal in teaching Heart Dances™ is to enhance your experience of the Lords' Prayer, which in turn enhances every aspect of your life. What I will show you here is how you may experience a melding of the eight pure spirits of these Heart Dances™ with the Lords' prayer in a simple exercise. It takes less than four minutes, but I can promise you this: If you will take just four minutes at least twice a day (eight minutes) your health, productivity and relationships will all improve. And the more present you are and the more often you are willing and able to do this simple exercise the more your life will improve.

"Kids: they dance before they learn there is anything that isn't music.

~*William Stafford*

REVIEW

To prepare you to get the most from this four-minute exercise I will briefly review what I have shared with you thus far. As we review Parts I thru VII, I will suggest some simple exercises to help you prepare for this simple four-minute experience. As we review keep in mind that this material is full of information that will help you to go more deeply and therefore enable you to receive more from this experience. If you are one who really takes this experience to heart and want to go as far and as deeply as possible with it then you may want to reread the entire book as it is full of subtle insights and information that will enable you to experience the Lord's Prayer as we do.

PART I: (THE INNER-CHILD)

It all began for us when we remembered and shared our childhood experiences of the Lord's Prayer in 1982. Beginning this way has always kept us mindful that this prayer has a lot to do with what Jesus said in Matthew 18:3 *"Except ye be converted, and become as little children, ye shall not enter into the kingdom of heaven. 18:5 And whosoever shall receive one such little child in my name receiveth me."* We believe that the first little child that we all must receive, and love is the one within us who is so crucial to our spiritual development.

Here we find an agreement with the first thing that Jesus taught: *"Repent for the kingdom of God is at hand."* The nature of a child is to be present. Children live in the here and now, which makes perfect sense, as Our Creator is omnipresent. This new experience of the Lord's Prayer begins as we simply pray to be fully present:

Say "OUR FATHER": Connecting with your Inner Source.

Say "IN HEAVEN: Looking within the present.

Say "HALLOWED BE THY NAME": Listening.

Say "THY KINGDOM COME, THY WILL BE DONE, AS IT IS IN HEAVEN SO ALSO IN EARTH": Assuming God's will is that we be present with Him now.

Say "GIVE US THIS DAY OUR DAILY BREAD": Opening to receive this day.

Say "AND FORGIVE US OUR TRESPASSES AS WE FORGIVE THOSE WHO TRESPASS AGAINST US": Releasing the past.

Say "AND LEAD US NOT INTO TEMPTATION BUT DELIVER US FROM EVIL": Letting go.

Say "AMEN", "it is done," knowing that the "Blessings already are."

PART II: (YOGA AND UNITY)

The idea that Jesus' message and the intent of his prayer are simply to help us be more present reminds us of what the Yogis of Far East teach. Looking at the Lord's Prayer as a form of yoga we observe the natural breathing

THE LORD'S PRAYER

Our *(in)* 1. Father *(out)*

Who art *(in)* 2. In Heaven *(out)*

Hallowed be *(in)* 3. Thy Name *(out)*

*Thy Kingdom *(in)* 4. Come *(out)*

*Thy Will *(in)* 4. Be Done *(out)*

*As it is in Heaven *(in)* 4. So also in Earth *(out)*

Give us This Day *(in)* 5. Our Daily Bread *(out)*

& Forgive us *(in)* 6. As we Forgive *(out)*

& Lead us not 7. into Temptation *(in)*

but Deliver us from Evil *(out)*

Amen*(in)* 8. Amen *(out)*

rhythm of its words and their associations with our seven chakra energy centers. Breathing deeply and fully as we pray, while focusing on these centers, naturally helps us to come into the present.

PART III: PLAYING "THE GAME"

The game, which has played such an important role in our understanding of the Lord's Prayer, is not really our creation. It was already there. We recognized it when we saw within correlations of the Lord's Prayer, the chakras and the original branches of yoga, plus an unexpected connection to our sixteen children's characters. How these pieces all fit together will be clear once we introduce the Heart Dances™. For the moment however, to alleviate your curiosity and because the first dance, the "Dance of Desire" is the foundation of all the others, I will share it with you now.

"The Dance of Desire," comes from the last segment of the prayer, "Lead us not into temptation but deliver us from evil." The steps of the first dance are "I am **receiving** (Terra), I am **giving** (Greedie), I am **wanting,** and I am **letting-go**." We all experience this first dance within every breath: "I am receiving **(in breath)**, I am giving **(out breath)**, I am wanting **(in)** and I am letting-go **(out).**" Do this a few times.

In every dance the fourth step or word is the key to our growth. For example, in this first dance the more we let go the more we may receive and the more we receive the more we can give. The more we give the more we want. The more we want the more we have to let-go of but again letting-go is the key. Receiving, giving and wanting all happen very naturally but how and when we choose to let go is up us.

As this dance is our foundation and since letting-go is the key to it, we all must ask ourselves what we have to let-go of. Generally, the answer is "attachment and resistance". By just looking at the first step or word of this first dance, you may reflect right now on what you may have to let go of. The first step is "Receiving," so think of what you are receiving. Now reflect on what you like receiving and what you do not like receiving. Think of what you are happy that you are not receiving and what you would like to receive but aren't. Do you see how many different feelings and relationships are bound to your experiences of receiving? I haven't even mentioned how you feel about what "they," the people in your life are receiving or not receiving and receiving is just the first of the 32 words or steps, which make up all eight of our Heart Dances™.

If we can agree our objective in the "Game of Life" is to be as free to be our true loving selves, then you may understand how our game helps us accomplish this. Receiving is an actual quality of our human spirit so our attachments and resistance to receiving naturally limit us. Heart Dances™ liberate our human spirits as they help us to release the fears and or doubts, which prevent us from being fully and unconditionally receiving.

PART IV: THE "ANCIENT ONES"

It is impossible to describe what we gained on our trip to Mexico. Even now Barbara and I don't fully understand what happened to us there. We certainly got a much stronger sense of the magnitude and timing of our human journey. Practically speaking however, we brought home from Mexico an amazing map of human consciousness called the "Sun Cross Codex". At the heart of both the Sun Cross Codex and the Lord's Prayer we find the same "sacrifice," which is another word for letting go. Growing up I was a surfer; Barbara was a dancer and these early passions also prepared us to understand the exquisite experience of surrendering to something greater. It is with this understanding that we have discovered and developed Heart Dances™.

What we surrender to in these Heart Dances™ is our own true and naturally free creator spirit. You can feel this right now in the first dance: "I am receiving **(in breath)**, I am giving **(out breath)**, I am wanting **(in)** and I am letting-go **(out).**" If you will repeat this simple exercise while focusing on surrendering to the forces within you that these simple words represent, then you will feel your spirit growing lighter and brighter. This is the "Dance of Desire," because desire is the key. The more in touch we are with what we truly want the more we can really let go to receive, give and want even more. It's easy to give up what we don't care about but try letting go of something that is really important to you. Then you will get a taste of how liberating this inner dance can be.

PART V: "JESUS IS FAST"

Our discovery of the sacred science of letting go within the Lord's Prayer was inspired by the promise that our lives could be magical. The presence, first of chakras and then the two stars in the prayer seemed to emphasize that we are "The Light of the World" and this most of all is what Heart Dances help us to experience. Again, we use the first dance, "The Dance of Desire" as an example:

Think of how a flame naturally receives and gives, wants and let's go. Now go through the steps of this first dance ("I am receiving **(in breath)**, I am giving **(out breath)**, I am wanting **(in)** and I am letting-go **(out).**") and feel each step as an expression of your spirit or inner light. There is a specific connection between the eight-pointed star-tetrahedron and our eight basic Heart

Dances™. Connecting the chakras reveals this star in the prayer, Heart Dances™ are also associated with the chakras and again this will become much clearer as we reveal all eight Heart Dances™.

PART VI: "THE BLESSINGS ALREADY ARE"

The all-important and illusive issue of faith, which was the subject of Part VI, is critical to experiencing the promise of our lives. The challenge to have faith was expressed by Jesus in many ways. My personal favorites are: "Seek first the kingdom of God and all these things shall be add unto you." "Repent for the kingdom of God is at hand." "Seek neither here nor there for the kingdom of God is within you." And, "Love God with all your heart, mind and spirit." Each of these expressions of faith illuminates "The blessings that already are" differently. "The blessings already are" is the key.

I know I said letting-go was the key but our faith that "The blessings already are," is what enables us to let-go. Wherever you are resistant to letting go you will find your faith that "The blessings already are" is lacking. So, to get the most from the Lord's Prayer and or these Heart Dances™ it is most important to exercise and evolve our faith that "The blessings already are" present within every facet of our lives. Be mindful of what is really important to you, what you really care about and what you really want. It makes no difference how impossible, trivial or absurd it may seem. Ask or pray like this: "Lord this is what I want, this or something better for my highest good" and let it go. Can you see how letting go opens us to receive? This is what Heart Dances™ do, they simply identify and guide us through all ways that we can let go to receive the blessings that are present for us here and now.

PART VII: HEART DANCES

BARBARA: For most of the past twenty-five years as our relationship with Jesus and his prayer has been evolving. Bodie was the active ingredient in our co-creative process. A few years ago, that changed when he came to me and said, "The Lord's Prayer and everything I know about the Lord's Prayer seems to be telling me to let go and I think I see a new way of doing that." Then he guided me through a very simple, very unusual and very powerful short meditation. It was a sequence of four simple affirmations, and I knew where they came from. These four affirmations obviously came from the first level of our game, but I'd never experienced, nor thought of experiencing it, that way before. When he saw that I was getting it he guided me through seven more of these meditations. Each flowed beautifully into the next and they all came from our game.

Bodie guided me through all eight of these little meditations in just a few minutes. When he was done, I was surprised at how light and good I felt. It was the way the Lord's Prayer makes me feel but I got there faster. As I was still relishing this experience with my eyes closed, I saw my goddess, the one from my vision at Temple of the Sun. With all eight of her dancing arms she pointed to her heart and I understood. A smile came over my whole body. I opened my eyes and I said, "Bodie these are dances! They are Heart Dances." Then I watched as the same big smile came over him and he said, "It's like surfing love."

Like Bodie there came a time in my life when I felt I had to leave my passion for dancing behind even though I still thought of myself as a dancer. I could watch great dancers and ice skaters for hours. My passion for the Lord's Prayer and my respect for Bodies unusual life and way of thinking always kept me interested and supportive of his creative process. But it was seeing and feeling this graphic expression of these eight dances within the game, which came to us from the prayer that engaged me fully and helped me to see how important my influence and contributions to this work really were.

"Creativity requires the courage to let go of certainties".

Eric Fromm

BODIE: Before we describe how these Heart Dances™ have come through a melding of the prayer, chakras, seven branches of yoga and our characters I must remind you that the characters are colored by our human prejudice for the positive and against the negative. When I say "positive" people generally hear "good." When I say "negative" they hear "bad" but "positive" and "negative" are really just indications of the direction that energy is flowing. An in breath for example would be "positive" as it is expansive, and an out breath is negative because it is contractive, but we can't have one without the other. Everything has a positive and negative side to it. In the first dance "Terra" (giving), who is the "positive" one is more appealing to us than the "Greedie" (receiving or taking) because he is the "negative" one.

We even have this saying that "There are two kinds of people in the world the givers and takers." The inference here is that the givers are the good guys and the takers are bad. In truth however, these two are of equal importance and value. If we don't receive ("Greedie") then we can't give ("Terra"). What is emphasized in the way that we have created these characters is not how God created us but how the prejudices of our will (ego) interfere with what God has created.

This is how and why these Heart Dances™ work. As you will see there's a wonderful balancing of opposites in each Heart Dance, which diminishes the linear projections of our ego/will. This is how Heart Dances™ reduce the imbalances of our ego/will by dissolving our habitual patterns of attachment and or resistance to the Divine Light within us.

The first two steps or words of each dance come directly from the characters. They identify the primary polarities or forces involved. The third word in every dance is where these forces tend to collide, as they do not agree. For example, in the first dance "Terra" (giving) and "Greedie" (receiving) both want something different. Wanting, the third step is where we generally get stuck until we can let go. The fourth word in each dance, is a unique and different expression of letting go which is the key. The more we can let go the more we may receive Our Father's love. So now, let us begin again with the first dance, "The Dance of Desire."

The 1ˢᵗ Dance:
DANCE OF DESIRE
"Receiving, Giving, Wanting & Letting-go"
"AND LEAD US NOT INTO TEMPTATION BUT DELIVER US FROM EVIL"

THE BASE CHAKRA
or "Sexual Center" is the "root" of our "sexual", life forces. We experience these forces as "desire," passion or hunger and their source is "The All-Consuming Flame", Our Creator who is within us. He/She is The Source of our free will, which is easily misdirected towards false promises or "temptations" on this most basic or primal level of our human consciousness.

> *"Men are admitted into Heaven not because they have curbed & governed their Passions or have No Passions, but because they have Cultivated their Understandings. The Treasures of Heaven are not Negations of Passion, but Realities of Intellect, from which all the Passions Emanate Uncurbed in their Eternal Glory".*
>
> *William Blake*

TANTRA YOGA is often associated with sex, but "Tantra" simply means "more." The question is what is more? The purpose of Tantra, like this level of the Lord's Prayer is to liberate us from the "temptations" or distractions of our physical senses by redirecting our awareness towards the higher spiritual levels of fulfillment. "What is more?" "Less is more" as the more we let go of the more we can receive. More is not measured by what we can hold onto or possess. It is what flows through us that gives us a true experience of abundance and this is what Tantra teaches.

THE CHARACTERS: Tantra is about working the law, "As you give  (represented by "Terra") so shall you receive (the "Greedie"): The more we give of  ourselves by simply being present, the more open and able we are to receive. What we all want or "desire" is to receive and to give more. The flame of desire is the pure creative force, which consumes our lives and us until we learn to master it. We master our desires by returning them to their source, which is The Master of us all. He/She is Our Creator and it is by letting go by saying "Lord this or something better for my highest good" that we accomplish this.

"DANCE OF DESIRE" is "I am **receiving** (in breath**), giving** (out breath), **wanting** (in breath) and **letting-go** (out breath)." As you close your eyes and breathe your way through these four steps remember that letting go is the key. And it is our faith that God does indeed "lead us not into temptation but deliver us from evil (Illusion)," which enables us to really let go.

The 2nd Dance
DANCE OF KNOWING
"Discerning, Trusting, Knowing and Accepting"

"AND FORGIVE US OUR TRESPASSES AS WE FORGIVE THOSE WHO TRESPASS AGAINST US"

NAVEL CHAKRA is the center where we digest and assimilate our "Daily Bread." To digest and assimilate "This Day, Our Daily Bread" we must let go of the past, which we call "forgiveness."

JNANA YOGA is the yoga of discernment and knowing. Good discernment is "Good Judgment," which results in good choices. But "harsh judgment" also comes from discernment. Good discernment is determining what is good or best. You could say that good judgment is discerning "The blessings that already are." Harsh judgment, which causes us to become "judgmental," on the other hand, is discerning what is bad or wrong. The benefit of good judgment is the experience of being at the right place at the right time, which is The Truth. The cost of being judgmental is to always miss The Truth.

> *"What makes the angels, angels*
> *Is not that they are holier than men or devils*
> *But that they do not expect holiness from one*
> *another, But from God alone".*
> *William Blake*

THE CHARACTERS: We must let go of the past to **discern** (represented by the  "Guilty") and **accept ("Beamer")** the blessings that God is bestowing upon us now. This is the "Dance of knowing" and knowing (the "Guilty") what is right and or wrong is what prevents us from really experiencing this dance.

Therefore, opening to **accept** more than we **know** (the 'Guilty') enables us to **discern**, **trust** ("Beamer") and experience to know even more. **Accepting** is the purest form of forgiveness and ultimately, we must forgive ourselves for judging ourselves to fully accept ourselves or anyone else. When we say, "And forgive us our trespasses as we forgive those who trespass against us" in the spirit of accepting we liberate ourselves from our past, to live in the present by accepting "The blessings which already are."

"It is impossible for a man to learn what he thinks he already knows".   *Epictetus*

DANCE OF KNOWING is "I am **discerning** (in breath), **trusting** (out breath), **knowing** (in breath) and **accepting** (out breath)." As you close your eyes now to breathe through these steps remember that accepting is the key to this dance. The more we can accept the more we can discern, trust and know and what sacrifice what we know we sacrifice to discern, trust and know even more.

The 3rd Dance
DANCE OF RESPONDING
"Unhappy, Happy, Responding and Appreciating"
"GIVE US THIS DAY OUR DAILY BREAD"

SOLAR PLEXUS, the largest muscle in the body, is located over our stomach or "breadbasket". This is the emotional Power Center where our feelings concerning survival, comfort, and issues of fairness all reside.

KARMA YOGA is characterized by learning to appreciate that we, as creators, are responsible for this "daily bread." Karma is a Sanskrit term meaning action or deed and "Karma" is the result of our physical deeds and thoughts. Karma Yoga teaches, just as Jesus did, "As you plant so shall you reap."

THE CHARACTERS: By praying, "Give us this day our daily bread," we accept creative **responsibility** (represented by the "Me Bear") for our actions. By reacting positively to what makes us **happy** ("We Bear") and negatively to what makes us unhappy

("Me Bear") we just perpetuate our current reality. Then we feel trapped and get bored which really makes us **unhappy** ("Me Bears"). We liberate ourselves to dance this dance by coming to appreciate the valuable gift that our "daily bread" represents. By **appreciating** both what we like and dislike as valuable insights for improving our lives we liberate ourselves to create something better. Happiness has no boundaries or limits, when it is not based on what happens but on who we truly are. We claim the freedom to simply be in the heavenly present by praying "Give us this day our daily bread." In the spirit of appreciation, we may assimilate the blessings of this day to create something better.

"Happiness is nothing more than good health and a bad memory."

Albert Schweitzer

DANCE OF RESPONDING is "I am **Unhappy** (in breath), **Happy** (out breath), **Responding** (in breath) and **Appreciating** (out breath)." Close your eyes now to breathe through these four steps and remember that appreciating is the key to this dance. The more we can appreciate the more we may experience both happiness and unhappiness as valuable guidance towards creating a better life from "The blessings already are."

The 4th Dance
DANCE OF CARING
"Repelling, Attracting, Caring and Grateful"
"THY KINGDOM COME, THY WILL BE DONE, AS IT IS IN HEAVEN SO ALSO IN EARTH"

HEART CHAKRA is our human center and the center of the Lord's Prayer. This is the pivotal point where heaven and earth either unite or become more divided within us.

BHAKTI YOGA is the yoga of devotion to God's will, love: "Do we open our hearts to love or defend them with walls of doubt and fear?" Bhakti Yoga is opening to experience gratitude for God's ever-present Loving will. In other words, through Bhakti yoga we devote ourselves to the realization that "The blessings already are."

THE CHARACTERS: "We are the light of the

world" because God who is The Light resides within us. His will, flows through our will **attracting** (represented by the "Luvvins"), what is for our highest good and **repelling** (the "Fearies"), what is not. A focused heart wills what we **care** about until it manifests, but our human hearts are frightened ("Fearies") and fickle. Our heartfelt fears, confusion and conflicts usually prevent us from focusing long enough to manifest anything much beyond the range of our "normal" experiences. Barbara's Café is an example of why that's generally a good thing. We may, however, rise above the limits of our human hearts by being **grateful** for everything. By saying "Thank you Lord" for absolutely everything, we affirm "The blessings that already are." As we align our willful hearts with God's heart/will, we stop interfering with how His heavenly love/will is attracting what is best and repelling what is not. "Thy kingdom come thy will be done as it is in heaven so also in earth." That's real magic.

*"Let us rise up and be thankful, for if we didn't
learn a lot today, at least we learned a little, and if
we didn't learn a little, at least we didn't get sick,
and if we got sick, at least we didn't die; so, let us
all be thankful".*

Buddha

DANCE OF CARING is "I am **repelling** (in
breath), **attracting** (out breath), **caring** (in breath) and
grateful (out breath)." In the spirit of gratitude, we are
naturally more present and therefore more capable of
receiving Our Father's love for us. As you close your eyes
now to breathe through these four steps remember that
feeling grateful is the key to this dance. The more grateful
you feel the freer you will be to experience "The blessings
that already are."

The 5th Dance
DANCE OF COMMUNING
"Listening, Speaking, Communing and Joyful"
"HALLOWED BE THY NAME"

THROAT CHAKRA is our center of
communication via listening and speaking. As we turn our
thoughts and words to God's presence, our attention
follows. Or, "As we think, in our hearts we shall become."

MANTRA YOGA is the practice of chanting
"mantras," which are special words formulated to express
or resonate to God's Holy Name ("The Word").

"Yahweh," "Om," "Hu," and "Sat Nam" are some of the most commonly known mantras. First we chant His name and then we listen for His response with the intent of experiencing divine Holy Communion." It is believed that such "mantras" can actually transform us.

OM MANTRA

The yogis who teach Mantra Yoga describe a "Holy River of Sound," a "Sacred Sound Current," emanating from God's heart that supports, loves, and nurtures everyone and everything. Moses described something similar when he said, "In the beginning was The Word and The Word was with God and The Word was God." Jesus also said: "Man does not live by bread alone but by every word from the mouth of God." Now even our scientists are discovering a subatomic sound coming for everywhere all at once.

CHARACTERS: As our journey began, we recognized the teaching of Mantra Yoga as the third attunement of the Lord's Prayer "Hallowed be thy name." Believing that as we **speak** ("+ Be Good Beagle") and **listen** ("- Be Good Beagle") with the intent of actually **communing** with God brings us **joy** in the realization of God's Holy Spirit residing within us.

DANCE OF COMMUNING is "I am **listening** (in breath), **speaking** (out breath), **communing** (in breath) and **joyful** (out breath)." As you close your eyes now to breathe through these four steps remember that feeling joyful is the key to this dance. The more we get in touch with the joy within us the more we will be in communion with Our Creator. Listen and speak with this intent and your heart will follow. This is a best and most rewarding way I know to experience "Ask and you shall receive." In communion with God we become aware that "The blessings already are," in a whole new way.

The 6th Dance
DANCE OF SEEKING/SEEING
"Negating, Affirming, Seeking/Seeing and Peaceful"
"WHO ART IN HEAVEN"

THE THIRD EYE in the center of our forehead is described by Eastern yogis as the window to the heavens. This chakra is where many Eastern teachers often instruct us to focus our attention while chanting or meditating. Many believe that Jesus was referring to this spiritual "eye" when he said, "Let your eye be single and your whole body is filled with light."

> *"The moment one gives close attention to anything, even a blade of grass, it becomes a mysterious, awesome, indescribably magnificent world in itself."*
>
> *Henry Miller*

Yantra Yoga, utilizes interlocking matrices of geometric patterns, that are magnificent visual designs called "yantras," which are specifically formulated to open the "Third Eye". Yantras do for our visual sense what mantras do for our hearing sense.

The "Sri Yantra" (below) is a visual expression of the "Om" mantra. By observing it objectively as a witness, without any judgment, making no comparisons and apply no meaning to it, you may actually feel how it lifts or shifts your awareness. By just observing this design and letting it move your awareness you will begin to feel more present. Focus long enough and you may actually experience  the fluid, ever changing unified field of omni-conditional awareness. Some say that in this state of awareness we penetrate the holographic fabric of light with which God creates and sustains our universe.

"Nature abhors a vacuum, and if I can only walk with sufficient carelessness, I am sure to be filled."
Henry David Thoreau

THE CHARACTERS: Jesus said that he spoke in parables because "they look but do not see and hear but do not listen or understand." Matthew 13: 13. The first thing he said was that heaven is "At hand" but we do not see it when we are looking for something else. We say, "Beauty is in the eye of the beholder" because we all see what we believe. We **negate** (represented by the "Bottomless Pit")

 and devalue what we do not want to see while **affirming** (the "Luv Crystal") and valuing what we do want to see. And what we all want to see is what we believe not

necessarily because that's what we like or want but because being right makes us feel safe and secure.

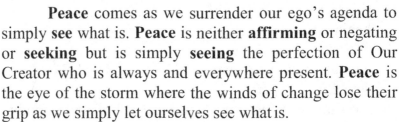

"If the doors of perception were cleansed, everything would appear to man as it is, infinite."   William Blake

Peace comes as we surrender our ego's agenda to simply **see** what is. **Peace** is neither **affirming** or negating or **seeking** but is simply **seeing** the perfection of Our Creator who is always and everywhere present. **Peace** is the eye of the storm where the winds of change lose their grip as we simply let ourselves see what is.

THE DANCE OF SEEING is "I am **negating** (in breath), I am **affirming** (out breath), I am **seeking/seeing** (in breath) and I am **peaceful** (out breath)." As you close your eyes now to breathe through these four steps remember that feeling peaceful is the key to this dance. The more we get in touch with our own peaceful center the more we see God's presence within and all around us. Trusting that the blessings already are is how we let your eye be single. Seeing everything, as a blessing is how we open our minds eye to The Truth, which sets us free.

The 7th Dance
DANCE OF ACCOMPLISHING
"Controlling, Liberating, Accomplishing and Free"
"OUR FATHER"

Crown Chakra is where we wear the "hat" that identifies us. This "hat" is generally associated with what we do, our work and our worldly accomplishments. In truth however, we are God's children. We are His accomplishment and nothing we do will add or detract from this.

Raja Yoga the "Royal Yoga" teaches us to exercise self-respect by honoring our body as our temple. As God's children, Our Father is "The King of all Kings" and we are His royal family. In Revelations 5: 10 it says, "And hast made us unto our God kings and priests: and we shall reign on the earth." This is what Raja Yoga teaches. We receive this authority by accepting creative responsibility for our own lives and by honoring every other persons right and obligation to do the same.

"Freedom is not worth having if it does not connote freedom to err".   Mohandas K. Gandhi

 **THE CHARACTERS:** Being royal is about **controlling** (represented by the "Sleeze") or focusing our creative awareness in ways that **liberate** (the "True Self") us, to be all that we can be. We honor  and express our "True Selves" by letting our inner light

shine. Jesus was affirming what we are to **accomplish** when he said, "You are the light of the world." He also said. "Ye are gods" and being **free** to express our God-given special-ness is the best possible way of, as William Shakespeare said, "To thyn own self be true." And, "Being true" is simply being present.

> *"When you meet someone better than yourself, turn your thoughts to becoming his equal. When you meet someone not as good as you are, look within and examine your own self".* *Confucius*

THE DANCE OF ACCOMPLISHING is "I am **controlling** (in), **liberating** (out, **accomplishing** (in) and I am **free** (out)." As you close your eyes now to breathe through these four steps remember that feeling free is the key to this dance. The freer we are to simply be, the more we will experience our divine/royal heritage as God's children. Controlling (focusing), our awareness to liberate ourselves by manifesting our own bliss is how we become free as we were indented us to be.

The 8th Dance

DANCE OF AWARENESS

"Consuming, Creating, Aware and Loving"

"OUR FATHER":

The Spiritual Heart is where God's Heart resides within us enveloping, caressing and supporting our own heart. As we say these first two words, "Our Father" we affirm who God is and He/She is Love.

Bhakti Yoga, the yoga of devotion is the yoga of both heart chakras. In the first one we devote our human hearts to Our Fathers loving will, as it manifests in our daily lives. Now in this second "Sacred Heart" we devote ourselves to His indwelling presence, within us. Jesus expressed the ultimate "Self-Realization," which comes from this highest devotion when he said, "I and my Father are One." I believe that to merge our small separate human identities with Our Father's universal identity (Unconditional Love) is the ultimate purpose of the Lord's Prayer.

THE CHARACTERS: Love is the indwelling riddle that humbles and lifts our **awareness** to worship the divine in all things. Love is the ultimate expression of freedom. It is the "All **Consuming F l a m e**" (represented by "Fear-on") and The  **Creator** (The "Father of Lights"). Love perfectly betrays every belief, relentlessly illuminating every flaw to the end, where in the beginning, the present betrays even natural law by returning more Love than was given. Love "delivers us from the illusion (evil) of separation until only The Truth of Love remains setting us free to simply be.

"...love comes from God. Everyone who loves has been born of God and knows God. Whoever does not love does not know God, because God is love." (1 John 4:7-8)

THE DANCE OF AWARENESS is "I am **consuming** (in breath), **creating** (out breath), **aware** (in breath) and I am **loving** (out breath)." As you close your eyes now to breathe through these four steps remember **loving** is the key to this dance. The more loving we feel the closer and more intimate we will be to Our Father. Consuming our lives with every in breath and creating life anew with every out breath is how we raise our awareness to the ultimate realization that each of us is a unique expression of Our Creator who is Love.

THE GAME

The information and experiences concerning these Heart Dances™ is also what our game contains. To experience a very simple version of this game simply choose an arbitrary method of selecting a number one through eight. You could use the numbers in the hat method or roll an eight-sided die as we do. Simply do this whenever you are feeling stuck or needing some guidance. Then re-read the information about the Heart Dance on the level which matches the number that you selected. If you will do this sincerely and only when you are truly feeling stuck, then I can guarantee that you will always receive something from these Heart-Dances™ that will help you to get more from your daily life experiences.

THE TWO-EDGED SWORD

In his vision of Christ on the island of Patmos the apostle John said: "And he had in his right hand **seven stars**: and out of his mouth went a sharp **two-edged sword**: and his countenance was as the sun shining in his strength" (Revelations 1: 16). We now see the Lord's Prayer is as John described, as this "two-edged sword." One edge of it is about us, the other is about God and its point is the ultimate promise expressed by Christ: "I and my Father are one." Our children's characters emphasize the two edges of this sword in a whole different way. They represent the polarities of our human consciousness and the points where these opposites unite are the eight steps to Unconditional Love.

In the "Dance of Desire" for example, receiving is one edge, giving is the other and wanting/desire brings us to the point of letting go to "deliverance." There were seven stars in the right hand of Christ but there are eight

Heart Dances because "his countenance was as the sun shining." The eighth star is "Loving" who is Christ and the point of this sword. The seven "stars" ascending to Him are the seven pure intentions or spirits within the Lord's Prayer that point us to Christ. They remind me of Jacob's vision of the "Ladder": *And he (Jacob) dreamed. And behold, a ladder set up on the earth, and the top of it reached to heaven. And behold, the angels of God ascending and descending on it"* (Genesis 28: 12).

THE MASTER DANCE
("THE DANCE OF ASCENSION")

To ascend the steps or spirits of this "ladder" is the point of our "Master Dance." It contains the final steps of all eight Heart Dances™. Hopefully you've taken the time

I AM *(in)* 8. LOVING *(out)*

I AM *(in)* 7. FREE *(out)*

I AM *(in)* 6. PEACEFUL *(out)*

I AM *(in)* 5. JOYFUL *(out)*

I AM *(in)* 4. GRATEFUL *(out)*

I AM *(in)* 3. APPRECIATING

I AM *(in)* 2. ACCEPTING *(out)*

I AM *(in)* 1. LETTING-GO *(out)*

"DANCE OF ASCENSION"

to breathe through and take in the blessings available to you. When you do so you can experience how uplifting these final steps are. Therefore, we often call this dance "The Dance of Ascension." In the next exercise you will experience each step or word as a radiant light or star affirming your own inner flame's spirit. See and feel how your flame expresses letting go, accepting, appreciating, gratitude, joy, peace, freedom and loving.

Affirm each of these eight lights while breathing into the appropriate chakra (see image "I Am in breath, Letting-go out breath etc.) reflect on how each is a pure expression of your own spirit.

IMPORTANT: We believe the basic intent of the Lord's Prayer is to guide us to the present, where God is. The more present you are, the more you will feel your radiance and the more you radiate the more present you will be.

PUTTING IT ALL TOGETHER

Now that we've gone through all the elements of our four-minute spiritual exercise let's put it all together. If you feel like your forgetting something or not getting it quite right just go back and re-read about that part. This short exercise is both very simple and yet complex. So, it will be easy to get started but remember like any exercise developing spiritual strength requires practice, patience and persistence. To make getting started as simple as possible we've put it all into just two illustrations on the next page. Just follow the instructions 1-8 in each image. Breathe and feel each word. First do the Dance then the prayer, and then reverse it. Feel how each word affirms the best in you. If you already know the Lord's Prayer, once you have memorized the eight simple words in the Dance of Ascension you will know it by heart. The dance and prayer together should take just four minutes.

I AM *(in)* 8. LOVING *(out)*
I AM *(in)* 7. FREE *(out)*
I AM *(in)* 6. PEACEFUL *(out)*
I AM *(in)* 5. JOYFUL *(out)*
I AM *(in)* 4. GRATEFUL *(out)*
I AM *(in)* 3. APPRECIATING
I AM *(in)* 2. ACCEPTING *(out)*
I AM *(in)* 1. LETTING-GO *(out)*

"DANCE OF ASCENSION"

THE LORD'S PRAYER

Our *(in)* 1. Father *(out)*
Who art *(in)* 2. In Heaven *(out)*
Hallowed be *(in)* 3. Thy Name *(out)*
*Thy Kingdom *(in)* 4. Come *(out)*
*Thy Will *(in)* 4. Be Done *(out)*
*As it is in Heaven *(in)* 4. So also in Earth *(out)*
Give us This Day *(in)* 5. Our Daily Bread *(out)*
& Forgive us *(in)* 6. As we Forgive *(out)*
& Lead us not 7. into Temptation *(in)*
but Deliver us from Evil *(out)*
Amen *(in)* 8. Amen *(out)*

THE PURSUIT OF HAPPINESS

Ironically the solutions to the problems that our unhealthy selfishness creates must be solved by healthy selfishness. Can you answer this question: "What do you want?" It sounds simpler than it really is as the values of cultures; our religions, nations, traditions, friends and families all profoundly affect what we believe we need to be happy. Striving to experience unity by adopting the accepted values of the "norm" however doesn't work. To be whole and to know the wholeness of our human family we must be our own selves. Following our own hearts, learning our own life lessons and discovering our own unique path to true happiness reveals what our unique contribution to the whole really is.

Most of us believe that happiness must be earned and that to pursue happiness for happiness sake is "selfish," "egotistical" or just plain "crazy." Crazy? Happy people are healthier, less likely to abuse drugs or alcohol, are generally more generous and less apt to do battle with others. Happy people don't need to seek approval or compromise their values. In fact, happy people don't need much at all. Can you imagine a world full of happy people? Jesus could and I am certain that's why he taught the Lord's Prayer. God has blessed each of us with the freedom to manifest our own unique lives and our own unique brand of happiness but most of us are afraid to express our unique God-given gifts. To be ourselves we must be "selfish" but in a good way.

As you pray:

"Our Father, who art in heaven, holy is your name. Thy kingdom come, thy will be done, as it is in heaven so also in earth, give us this day our daily bread and forgive us our trespasses as we forgive those who trespass against us and lead us not into temptation but deliver us from evil, Amen."

Hear these simple words encouraging you to be all that you can be? Can you hear Jesus saying, "To realize your dreams you must simply be yourself?"

THE BOOK OF LIFE

I was nearly finished with this book and feeling very good about how it had come together when something unexpected happened. As you know, this book represents a culmination of twenty-five years of working, seeking and sharing the promise within the Lord's Prayer. I should be elated by this accomplishment, but I felt like something was missing. I had no idea what it was, and I was so close to completion. It didn't make any sense, but I just couldn't finish. I felt disconnected from the wonderfully full, exciting and meaningful journey that I have been sharing with you here. I prayed for understanding and saw that part of me was afraid. Would completing this book end this journey? I didn't know but I knew I had to finish it and then something happened.

One day our son, Azza, brought home a very special book. It was one of those nice artists books with heavy paper for illustrations, and what made it special was not just what was on those pages. This book was a communal expression of heart. It had been passed from one creative person to the next and on each page were original heartfelt drawings, stories, poems, collages or some combination of these. Each person had obviously expressed his or herself passionately and then just let it go to the next person. That's what was so beautiful about it. The trust which was obviously required that each person would respect and care for this precious collection of dancing hearts.

Its pages were nearly all full when it was given to Azza, who was then 17, to make his contribution. It was worn the way books are when they have been shared, read and cared for by many people. As I looked through it what I saw was courageous, true beauty obviously poured from vulnerable, exposed hearts. I was deeply moved by their collective creative effort and as I held it, I felt a strong sense of yearning. I have been so fortunate to have this co-creative relationship with Barbara, but I often imagine what it would be like to have many souls so united as they were in this special book. Many of these people didn't even know one another and this too added to the beauty and mystery of it.

That night I dreamt about that book. I saw it being passed amongst these caring people and again I felt the yearning. The bond I felt between them was strong and sweet with mutual respect and admiration. Then unexpectedly one of them passed it to me. Instead of feeling honored I felt unworthy. What could I contribute to such a splendid relationship? I found a blank page with my name and I felt trapped. It was a familiar feeling of knowing that no matter what I did "It" would not be good enough. Then the words Heart Dances appeared on my page. I felt a great release and I began writing and when I had finished, I closed it and on the cover it said, "The Book of Life."

As I held this book in my dreams my hands were trembling as my heart was pounding. For the first time I saw "Heart Dances" as my contribution to that great book. I remembered how the nuns had told us that in "The End" our sins would be recorded and read to all from the "Book of Life." For some reason the great embarrassment that I imagined would be the end result of this event was even more frightening to me than eternal damnation in Hells fire. In this dream, I saw it all differently. I saw that the "Book of Life" was a record of our contributions and how each person's contribution was their own self.

After this dream I felt complete. I knew that my life was good, and I had no doubts about anything at all. I woke up full of this good feeling and I knew that I could finish this book. I saw how this ending is also a beginning and how the Lord's Prayer draws from each us our own unique contribution to this life.

TAKE THE OATH

I first experienced the power of an oath when I took Peter Pan's Oath to "Never Grow Up." Gratefully fifty-four years later Peter's oath is still with me as I do take such delight in playing with our grandchildren. On my fourth birthday I took Peter's oath in the presence of a whole theater full of witnesses and I believe that's part of what made it so powerful. I believe my age was also a factor. Four-year olds are very impressionable and that is the approximate age of development attributed to our inner child. I also believe that to receive the full benefit of the Lord's Prayer it should be expressed as a sacred oath to our own selves with God and our spiritual family as our witnesses.

The first thing Doris asked me when I became her client was "Why do you want to do this? What do you hope to gain from this work that we will be doing together?" That was the lowest point of my life. I believed, as I'd been told, that the damage I'd done to myself with drugs and starvation would leave me permanently handicapped for the rest of my life. So, I answered Doris' question by saying, "I just want to be the best person I can be." Years later Doris said that she'd asked that question of all her clients and that my answer was the best she'd heard.

Today my best understanding of the promise of the Lord's Prayer is that if we will just follow the simple steps that it lays out, we will be the best person we can be. When I hear Jesus say, "Seek first the kingdom of God and all these things shall be added unto you," I hear that "Our Father supports us generously in our true pursuits of happiness." When he said, "Repent for the kingdom of God is at hand," I hear him saying, "Be here now" and I believe this is what the heart of the Lord's Prayer: "Thy kingdom come, thy will be done, as it is in heaven, so also in earth," is all about. I believe God wants us to be happy and that "The blessings already are". The Lord's Prayer is a sacred oath masterfully designed to help us do just that.

If the only prayer you said in your whole life was,
"Thank you", that would suffice.
Meister Eckhart

I believe we all "miss the mark" (happiness) by putting off our dreams as we avoid taking our sacred oath to be all that we can be. "The kingdom of God is at hand; the time is now" and the Lord's oath encourages us to be present in communion with God and each other. Praying this way, as His holy family, we stop living and thinking as isolated beings. As we assume "The blessings already are" by silently saying "Thank you," "I love you" and "God bless you," to everyone and everything that draws our attention helps reveal the blessings and lift the heart. This magical way of living is The Promise that I felt when I was seven, saying the Lord's Prayer, and I still do!

> *"All it takes is faith and trust,*
> *Oh and something I forgot,*
> *Just a little bit of pixie dust"*
>
> *Peter pan*

A LONG AND WINDING ROAD

I was seventeen and selling woman's shoes in a Leeds Shoe Store, when my kindergarten teacher, whom I hadn't seen since I was five, sat down in my section. Just to be sure, I asked, "Is your name Mrs. Wiern?" She looked a bit surprised, smiled kindly, and said, "Yes, how did you know that?" I told her that she had been my kindergarten teacher, and she asked my name. As I replied, her smile faded, her body stiffened, and her eyes focused on mine. She looked very deliberately into my eyes and stated, "I thought you'd be dead or in prison by now." Then I think I sold her a pair of shoes!

It wasn't until years later, when my own children were in school, that I realized how unusual Mrs. Wiern's response to me was. What must have I done when I was five for her to be holding on to such feelings twelve years later? As I reflected on what I could remember of that kindergarten year, I recalled how excited I was to go to school, and then how disappointed I felt when it was not as I'd imagined. I also remembered that Mrs. Wiern had insisted that I be given a series of aptitude tests. When the results didn't match her expectations, she insisted that I be re-tested. Ultimately, these tests confirmed for my parents and future teachers that I was capable of great things. As you've read, they were all very disappointed in me for the next twelve years, and these tests added greatly to their frustration and mine. So, whatever it was that I might have done to Mrs. Wiern, she got her revenge.

At the beginning of every school year, I was asked by my teachers to stay after class to hear the same speech about how I could do anything that I wanted to. In all those years, however, no one ever asked me what I wanted to do. I am certain that, if only we would ask every child every day, "What do you want?" the quality of their lives and ours would undoubtedly improve immensely. True creative thinking comes as we surrender to the sacred flame of free will within us. Both our schools and churches value memorization over thinking, which slowly extinguishes our creative flame. They train us to become the cogs and wheels in the machinery of our society, and we are punished if we cannot or will not conform.

To avoid punishment in high school, I bought blank report cards and became pretty good at forgery; but I couldn't give myself the grades they expected without getting caught. Perhaps it was Peter Pan's oath that caused me to resist the traditional indoctrination of our culture. I graduated high school with a D+ average, and then a miracle happened--my SAT scores got me into the University of San Diego, and I had to endure one more semester of torment. My scholastic struggle was suspended for seventeen years until I began writing about this work, at which time I had to face all the fears and resistance that I developed during those thirteen years in public school.

Fortunately, the years of working with my inner child were very helpful. It wasn't so much a process of trying to do something that I wasn't very good at. Instead, it was a very deep and personal experience of healing this inner child by helping him to see his value as creator. We began healing these old wounds by associating the great task of writing a book with pleasure. Each morning, he and I went to the Rose Café in Venice Beach for scones and coffee. Munching and sipping and writing in such a wonderfully creative environment, we quickly overcame our resistance. What took the longest was not overcoming our fears of failure, but instead the comfort of the process.

As this long and winding road finally brought me to completion, I felt that I was finishing a Special Olympics marathon. My handicap hadn't stopped me. I'd done my personal best; but, as I crossed that finish line, I also felt that something was missing. Sarah, our editor, was very reassuring; but I knew I'd left something very important out of my book. I had gone straight from writing to stressing over a website, DVD, and the other things I imagined we would need to promote and sell this book - but wasn't there supposed to be a celebration, or something? Instead of the better, richer life I imagined, I saw a life more complex and challenging. Then I remembered what my friend Gilo said about Barbara's Café, "So Bodie, you did all this work to create a harder job for yourself?"

SMILE

I was going through this final torment and feeling a bit lost, when Barbara turned on Oprah. Her guest was Elizabeth Gilbert, the author of the bestselling book, *Eat,*

Pray, Love. I thought perhaps this accomplished author would shed some insight on what to do once a book is complete. I saw how many of Elizabeth's experiences and insights paralleled my own; but when she started talking about a man that she met in Bali, I found myself listening very intently. It was as though something within me knew she was about to reveal the gem of wisdom I needed at that very moment.

Elizabeth was talking to the Balinese man about her experiences with meditation at an ashram in India, when he said that he didn't understand why the Indian Yogis made meditation so complicated. He told her to try just sitting and smiling with every part of herself, "even with your liver." When he said this, I began to smile; and I saw and felt all the brilliant smiles I'd experienced on this long journey. I realized how those many smiles along the way were as important as completing this book, and how I much I'd come to love this journey. Part of me was afraid that perhaps the magic might also be complete, but magic never is. A smile is how we experience blessings that already are, and our blessings are endless. What is heaven if not a place of endless smiling? Every part of the Lord's Prayer points to an entire ocean of smiles.

I used to wake up each day thinking of all the things I had to do. Even before my eyes were open, I could feel my body starting to tense with the stress of my unfinished tasks. Then I thought about the smiling meditation and tried it for a few minutes. Next, I did it with the Lord's Prayer and with our Heart Dances™, and it was even better. Then I remembered something else Elizabeth had said: "Before you get out of bed each morning, think of something you want to do that day." I took her advice, and guess what? The things I wanted to do were the same things I was thinking I needed to do. However, while thinking I had to do them made me feel stressed and anxious, thinking of the things I wanted to do made me feel light and happy.

This experience reminded me of something that Doris used to say: "A person's healthy passion and the emotional illness which undermines it are identical in appearance." By this, she meant that the very things that make us feel most alive are also how we avoid living. I wrote this book to share what I love. It is what I wanted to do but thinking of it as something that I had to do often robbed me of this great pleasure. There is a smile in everything and everyone whose goodness we are willing to savor. To attract something good, we must simply focus on something good. This wondrous creative freedom, Our Indwelling Creator's greatest gift to us, may also be used to manifest our fears. That is why the Lord's Prayer is such a valuable tool, as it so beautifully illuminates what we truly want.

This great two-edged sword called "The Lord's Prayer" points to the ultimate smile. In the East they call it "God consciousness." Jesus embodied and expressed it when he said, "*I and my Father are one.*" To commit ourselves to this ultimate goal, we must first believe it is possible. But if it weren't possible, why would Jesus have promised it in his prayer? The moment that I committed myself to discovering it, before I even knew what it was, my mundane life was transformed into a magical one. The job that I hated, waiting tables, became both rewarding and enjoyable. The distances between Barbara and me dissolved, and this is just one practical benefit of embracing this prayer—it elevates even our most mundane and sometimes distasteful tasks to enjoyable and rewarding ones.

As I've shared, I first experienced the power of an oath when I took Peter Pan's oath to "never grow up." Peter's oath made my heart smile; but this oath, the Lord's oath, makes every part of me smile and awakens parts I did not even know existed. As we embrace this ultimate promise of unconditional, heavenly happiness, we must be mindful that there is always more. The Promise has no end, and perhaps that has something to do with why ending this book was so challenging. The ultimate smile grows within us as we awaken to what it is that we really want. From there, it is simply a matter of *ask and you shall receive,* and there is always more. We open the eternal floodgates of joy by giving thanks for everything.

The blessings already are and the more present or open we are the more we may receive and know that we are blessed. "Thank you" opens the heart, "I love you" engages the heart, and with "God bless you" our hearts are united with God's heart and with His purpose. Silently express "Thank you, I love you, and God bless you" to everyone and everything, and you will see how quickly The Promise grows within you. And remember, there is always more.

"All it takes is faith and trust,
Oh and something I forgot,
Just a little bit of pixie dust"
Peter Pan

It takes *faith* in God's goodness and wisdom to say, "Thank you".

It takes *Trust* in the capacity of our own hearts to say, "I love you."

"God bless you" is the *"pixie dust"* that dissolves the illusion to reveal The Truth, and there is always more.

Take the Oath, Live the Promise
& Know the Lord's magic!

Our Father
Who art in Heaven.
Hallowed be Thy Name.
Thy Kingdom come, Thy
Will be done on Earth as it is in
Heaven. Give us this day our dai-
ly bread and Forgive us our tres-
passes, as we forgive those who
trespass against us. Lead us
not into temptation, but
deliver us from evil.
Amen

To learn more, go to seeyourselfloving.com

ILLUSTRATIONS

Listed in order of appearance.

RECOMMENDED READING

AUTOBIOGRAPHY OF A YOGI   By Parmahansa Yogananda

THE BIBLE   (King James Version)

BE HERE NOW   By Baba Ram Das

THE MURDER OF CHRIST   By Wilhelm Reich

THE FUNCTION OF THE ORGASM   By Wilhelm Reich

TRANSACTIONAL ANALYSIS   By Eric Bern

PRIMAL SCREAM Dr.   By Arthur Janov

CRITICAL PATH   By Buck Mister Fuller

THE LORD'S PRAYER   By Ralph M. De Bitt

THE ILLUSTRATED I CHING   By R. L. Wing

THE GOLDEN DAWN   By Israel Regardie

THE MAYAN FACTOR   By José Argüelles

SURFERS OF THE ZUVUYA   By José Argüelles

HOLOGRAPHIC UNIVERSE   By Michel Talbot

COSMIC TRIGGER   By Robert A. Wilson

THE ANCIENT SECRETS OF THE FLOWER OF LIFE,

VOLUMES I & II   By Drunvalo Melchizedek

BLESSINGS OF LIGHT   By John Roger

THE WAY OUT BOOK   By John Roger

SPIRITUAL WARRIOR   By John Roger

FULFILLING YOUR SPIRITUAL PROMISE by John Roger

THE BLESSINGS ALREADY ARE   By John Morton

THE POWER OF NOW   By Eckhart Tole

PRISON TO PRAISE   By Merlin R. Carothers

Made in the USA
Middletown, DE
22 July 2024